COLLEGE ESSAY CONFIDENCE

Also by Jill Margaret Shulman

College Admissions Cracked:
Saving Your Kid (and Yourself) from the Madness

Praise for *College Essay Confidence*

"*College Essay Confidence* is the reassuring, wise, and often hilarious step-by-step guide every college applicant needs. With her relatable voice and chill attitude, Jill Margaret Shulman offers clever strategies, catchy mantras, fun facts, real examples, and practical techniques that empower you to craft a personal essay that truly represents who you are. Shulman understands teens and knows how to demystify the writing process. Whether you need help choosing a topic or are unsure how to revise, reading *College Essay Confidence* feels like having the most knowledgeable writing coach by your side, cheering you on. As both a writer and a mom of a high school senior who just went through the college application process, I wish we'd had this book earlier!"

— **Rachel Rabkin Peachman**, coauthor of *When Children Feel Pain*

"This fun and motivating book offers the best skill-building and step-by-step strategies to help students face their dreaded personal essay. An added benefit is the huge boost to self-understanding, an essential component of mental health, which will only help the students when they arrive at college. *College Essay Confidence* lives up to its name and is highly recommended."

— **Mia Nosanow, MA, LP**, author of *The College Student's Guide to Mental Health*

"Jill Margaret Shulman brings her insight and expertise (and some much-needed humor) to what can feel quite overwhelming and anxiety-producing. Her approach doesn't just help students write stronger essays; it nurtures confidence, calm, and authenticity along the way. I wish *College Essay Confidence* had been there for my children when they were applying to college!"

— **Cheryl Vigder Brause**, mindfulness instructor and cofounder of pausetobepresent.com

"Jill Margaret Shulman coaches aspiring college essay writers with personalized exercises and tools to develop confidence and to use their authentic voices. Her book guarantees a positive and successful essay writing experience."

— **Katie Fretwell**, former dean of admission and financial aid at Amherst College

"Jill Margaret Shulman's humorous, down-to-earth approach is a breath of fresh air. Brimming with clever brainstorming ideas, playful writing activities, and creative revision exercises, this book gives students the tools they need to tackle the writing process with confidence and optimism."

— **Jaime Smith, MA, MSEd, CEP**, author of *The Complete Guide to College Transfer*

"*College Essay Confidence* is a practical guide with wise information on how to find the power in your voice. And it delivers what it promises. You will write a *knockout* application essay!"

— **Nancy Slonim Aronie**, author of *Writing from the Heart*, *Memoir as Medicine*, and *Seven Secrets to the Perfect Personal Essay*

"Teens applying to college get lots of advice from lots of places, especially about the personal essay. Much of it is misinformed, full of clichés, or flat-out wrong. Jill Margaret Shulman (a true expert) has seen this for decades, so she wrote a book that busts myths and offers solid steps to take, from working through a messy first draft to receiving feedback from the right people. Parents, hand this book to your teen and step back. Jill knows her stuff."

— **Lynn Lyons**, anxiety expert, coauthor of *Anxious Kids, Anxious Parents*, and host of the *Flusterclux* podcast

Conquer Blocks, Free Your Voice, and Write a **Knockout** Application Essay

Jill Margaret Shulman

New World Library
Novato, California

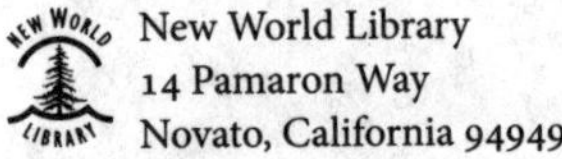
New World Library
14 Pamaron Way
Novato, California 94949

Text design by Tona Pearce Myers

Library of Congress Cataloging-in-Publication data is available.

First printing, January 2026
ISBN 978-1-955831-06-2
Ebook ISBN 978-1-955831-07-9
Printed in Canada

10 9 8 7 6 5 4 3 2 1

New World Library is committed to protecting our natural environment. This book is made of material from well-managed FSC®-certified forests and other controlled sources.

Contents

Introduction

The Secret to Writing (and World) Domination

Tyler breezed into my office at 1:02 p.m. for our 1:00 meeting. "Sorry I'm a little late. The traffic on Route 9 was horrible," he said.

"No worries. I'm impressed you made it," I said, and I meant it because the construction on Route 9 that summer was no joke.

Tyler eased into the blue velvet comfy chair facing my desk. He removed the throw pillow from behind his back because who needs a throw pillow when you're ten feet tall? I exaggerate, but Tyler qualified for the Tall Clubs International Foundation college scholarship, for which you, too, can apply if you're over 5′10″ (and female) or 6′2″ (and male). Truth.

"Just set the pillow on the floor," I said, and Tyler did, then returned to his full upright position, head floating above the chair's upholstery, denim-covered knees jutting out far beyond the edge of the seat.

Tyler couldn't have looked more at ease. He combed his fingers through his thick black hair, which bounced back into place in perfect formation like a platoon of obedient soldiers. I'd seen Tyler's résumé before our meeting, and his haircut was not the only thing about him that looked perfect. You know this guy. He's the one who is captain of the ice hockey team, president of student council, and in the running for valedictorian (so you've heard). At your school, Tyler might be called Alex or M.J. or Stella, but you get the idea. When you think of the person who has all the credentials colleges look for and will get in *everywhere* (everyone says so), Tyler is that person.

Then I said, "How are you feeling about writing your personal essay for your college application?"

It was as if I'd poked a sharp knife into the bubble of confidence surrounding Tyler. In the silence that followed, the guy everyone wants to be began to deflate until he slumped so low in the chair across from my desk, I was sure he'd disappear into the cushions if he could. His face drooped, betraying his downward-spiraling thoughts, along the lines of: *I'm going to tank this essay and never get into a good college or get a good job or become successful or happy in life.* No one wants to be Tyler at this moment, flattened by the prospect of writing an essay that he believed (as perhaps you believe) could make or break his future. "I'm kind of nervous," he finally said.

What I want you to know, right now at the start of our journey together toward your knockout college essay, is that I *see* you. You may or may not be the one spotlighted on the ice scoring goal after goal (or killing it at the debate podium or sitting in the front row raising your hand in class), but no one is 100 percent as they appear. You have an unlimited supply of transcendent, blindingly bright power equal to Tyler's. You also have that voice inside your head that insists on blasting you with hate talk and blocking your light. I call that voice your *Inner Troll.*

Regardless of what's visible to the outside world, and regardless of how you see yourself today, you are worthy and capable of writing a spectacular essay, getting into a good college, landing a good job, and having success and happiness in your life.

Confidence is the secret sauce to writing (and world) domination. (Cymbal crash.)

It sounds simple, but it's not. Achieving a confident mindset means truly believing you have the power, the ability, and the *right* to succeed, which is hard enough. Sustaining that headspace all the way through the writing process until you've produced a standout personal essay is the real challenge. In other words, the obstacles to crafting your college essay are all in your head. This book will take you by the hand and guide you step-by-step with instructions, advice, and Brain Boosters to keep your head screwed on straight, from the topic hunt through creation, revisions, and the final draft of your essay. I've shepherded students through this writing process for many years and evaluated countless applications as a college admission evaluator. I've got you covered. Along the way, you'll learn how to take control of your own future and communicate with impact. This is going to be empowering and fun (yes, *fun*)!

So back to Tyler. I gave him the same reality check and pep talk I just gave you, and he sat up straighter. By the end of our first meeting, he was excited instead of apprehensive to write in a new way he'd never tried before — that is, after he made it back home through all the Route 9 construction traffic. That day began Tyler's journey toward the knockout college essay you can read in the Appendix at the end of this book.

Preview of Your Writing Adventure Ahead

As you travel through these pages, you'll see lots of examples of the steps students who came before you took on their adventures through four drafts of their essays. Watch how my rough draft below progresses through each draft that follows, as words are subtracted (strikethrough) and added (underlined).

Draft 1: The Hot Mess (with Potential for Greatness)

This is my first draft of this preview, so I'd stop reading now, if I were you. Seriously. It will be a hot mess because that's the way with first drafts, all over the place, and for me specifically, writing first drafts means a whole lot of warm-up words before I get to the point, which is that you're gonna write a crappy first draft. We all do. Like I said, it will be a hot mess. No one will ever see it (I'm sharing mine with you because I'm a masochist), and so you can "write into" the story, as I generally do, you can make mistakes, fix them later, or you can start again the minute you finish, which I might do, and it's all good. The only way to write well is to take the risk that you won't, and the moral of this terribly written story is that when (not if) you don't write well, it's okay. It will all work out just fine after you've waded through four drafts, found your point, airbrushed all those mistakes away, and are ready to share your writing with the world. The end of the story is that you'll finish an essay you feel proud of, that really reflects the true you, you'll get into college, and that will be that. So now I'm going to end this charade of public humiliation and move on to the second draft of this preview in which I will try to cobble together the hidden gems within the rubble of this hot mess, shut up my Inner Troll (who is noisy and really really mean) that will tell me to start over! This is horrible! You have some ego to presume you can help anyone through writing their personal essay. You need help yourself! Anyway, by the time I journey through revisions, that voice will be a mere memory. You'll see.

Draft 2: The Big Picture

~~This is my first draft of this preview, so I'd stop reading now, if I were you. Seriously. It will be a hot mess because that's the way with first drafts, all over the place, and for me specifically, writing first drafts means a whole lot of warm-up words before I get to the point, which is that you're gonna write a crappy first draft. We all do. Like I said, it will be~~ As Promised, my draft one of this preview was a hot mess. ~~No one will ever see it (I'm sharing mine with you because I'm a masochist), and so you can "write into"~~

~~the story, as I generally do, you can make mistakes, fix them later, or you can start again the minute you finish, which I might do, and i~~It's all good because~~. T~~ the only way to write well is to take the risk that you won't write well.~~ , a~~And the moral of this terribly written story is that when (not if) you don't write well, it's okay. No one will ever see your first (or second or third) draft, and ~~I~~it will all work out ~~just fine~~ after you've waded through four drafts, found your point, airbrushed ~~all those~~ mistakes away, and are ready to share your writing with the world. The end of the story is that you'll finish an essay you feel proud of, that really reflects the true you, you'll get into college, and that will be that. ~~So now I'm going to end this charade of public humiliation and move on to the second draft of this preview in which I will try to cobble together the hidden gems within the rubble of this hot mess,~~ But at the start, to get anything at all on paper, you'll have to shut up ~~my~~ your Inner Troll, which can be ~~(who is~~ noisy and really, really mean~~)~~. Great news! ~~that will tell me to start over! This is horrible! You have some ego to presume you can help anyone through writing their personal essay. You need help yourself! Anyway, b~~By the time ~~I journey~~ you've traveled through revisions, that voice will be a mere memory. You'll see.

Draft 3: Sweat the Smaller Stuff

~~As Promised, my draft one of this preview was a hot mess.~~ Take it from me, a recovering perfectionist, it was not fun to look back on that cringey hot mess of a first draft, but with a little perspective (and a sense of humor), ~~I~~it's all good because the only way to write well is to take the risk that you won't ~~write well. And the moral of this terribly written story is that when (not if) you don't write well, it's okay~~. No one will ever see ~~your first (or second or third) draft~~ anything you write until you have~~, and it will all work out after you've~~ waded through four (or five or eight) drafts, found your point, ~~airbrushed~~ <u>fixed</u> mistakes ~~away~~, and are <u>good and</u> ready to share your writing with the world. <u>Now you can stop imbuing that first draft of your college essay with mystical powers.</u> The end of the story is that you'll finish an essay ~~you feel proud of~~, that ~~really~~ reflects the true you, you'll get into college, and that will be that. But at the start <u>of your writing journey</u>, to ~~get~~ <u>capture</u> anything at all on paper, you'll have to shut up your Inner Troll, which can be ~~noisy and~~ really, really mean. Great news! ~~By the time you've traveled through revisions, that voice will be a mere memory. You'll see.~~ <u>You've landed in the right place, in a world where Inner Trolls are not allowed, so you can figure out what you want to say and then say it with authenticity. More great news! You are not alone anymore. I've guided thousands of students through the personal essay writing adventure, and now I've got your back.</u>

Draft 4: Polish

~~Take it from me, a recovering perfectionist, it was not fun to look back on that cringey hot mess of a first draft, but with a little perspective (and a sense of humor), it's all good because the only way to write well is to take the risk that you won't. No one will ever see anything you write until you have waded through four (or five or eight) drafts, found your point, fixed mistakes, and are good and ready to share your writing with the world. Now you can stop imbuing that first draft of your college essay with mystical powers. The end of the story is that you'll finish an essay that reflects the true you, you'll get into college, and that will be that. But a~~<u>A</u>t the start of your writing journey, to capture anything at all on paper, you'll ~~have~~ <u>need</u> to shut up your Inner Troll~~,~~ <u>(</u>which can be really~~, really~~ mean<u>) and write badly</u>. <u>Take it from me, a recovering perfectionist, the only way to write well is to risk that you won't.</u> Great news! You've landed in ~~the right place, in~~ a world where Inner Trolls are ~~not allowed~~ <u>excommunicated</u>, so you can figure out what you want to say and then try to say it with authenticity. ~~More great news! You are not alone anymore.~~ I've guided thousands of students step-by-step through the personal essay writing adventure, and ~~now~~ you are not alone anymore. I've got your back.

The Final Draft

At the start of your writing journey, to capture anything at all on paper, you'll need to shut up your Inner Troll (which can be really mean) and write badly. Take it from me, a recovering perfectionist, the only way to write well is to risk that you won't. Great news! You've landed in a world where Inner Trolls are excommunicated, so you can figure out what you want to say and then try to say it with authenticity. I've guided thousands of students step-by-step through the personal essay writing adventure, and you are not alone anymore. I've got your back.

Cast of Characters

You now have me to provide skills and support for your essay writing adventure ahead, as well as a cast of characters already mucking around inside your brain (they have always lived there).

Your Inner Troll

We all have an Inner Troll, and it is the worst. Some people call it an Inner Critic, but not me. Criticism is not all bad, but your Inner Troll is the embodiment of evil. Its brand of criticism always undercuts but never enhances your excellence. Your Inner Troll is your archenemy, the villain in your essay writing adventure. Throughout this book, I've implanted tools to brandish like swords to fight the constant battle with your fierce Inner Troll (you are fiercer). I'll provide the sharpest blades at the points in the writing process when that Inner Troll of yours is most likely to appear for an unwelcome visit.

Your Inner Editor

I want to clarify from the start that your Inner Editor, while not always easy on you, will become your ally starting in draft 3 of your essay. It will save you from slipups that won't play well in the admissions office. But if your Inner Editor appears too early and starts to tempt you to edit *before* you write, that means your Inner Troll has corrupted it, so don't listen! In parts I and II of this book, your job is to write like no one will ever see it (they won't). Later, your Inner Editor can step in to consider your reader's reaction to what you've written and adjust accordingly.

Outside Voices

Over the years, your brain has absorbed countless thoughts and opinions from outside voices, some helpful, some not. Kick other people's voices out of your head as best you can, and by all means, don't invite any new ones in while you're getting started. Yours is the only voice that counts right now. At the very end of this writing process, all the way in chapter 13, you'll hand over your essay to some trusted readers who live outside your head before colleges read it. You'll give your chosen readers written guidelines that will prove important to help steer them toward constructive rather than destructive feedback. By then, you'll have completed enough Brain Boosters to shore up the courage to truly hear their feedback and weed out what's helpful from what is not.

Caution: If you invite others' opinions into the mix too soon, those outside voices will seep in and strengthen the voice of your Inner Troll. Then your fortified Inner Troll will have a field day sneaking around and undermining you *while posing as an ally.*

You will need your most trusted IRL advisers, but not yet. If you need assistance fending off prematurely and persistently curious would-be "helpers," flip directly to "Dragon Training" in chapter 6. You've got this.

Your Inner Superhero

Listen to your Inner Superhero from the beginning to the end of your essay writing journey. This is the angel who sits on your shoulder whispering, *You are confident and competent* (while your Inner Troll sits on your other shoulder whispering, *You're a bumbling buffoon*). The Brain Boosters will help you exile your Inner Troll, and they will also help you invoke your Inner Superhero to *encourage your courage* to win this battle and write your very best.

Your Inner Essayist

We're all capable of writing an extraordinary personal essay. Speaking your truth on the page takes more bravery than talent or skill. If your Inner Essayist (who is already inside you) is napping now, don't worry. This book will wake it up. Or perhaps your Inner Essayist is wide awake, eager for permission to help you say what you are burning to say once you expel your Inner Troll. I'm excited to help you awaken and motivate your Inner Essayist to support you as you write an essay that will sing, dance, and play the harmonica to make your college application stand out.

Part I

THE TOPIC HUNT

Chapter 1

Get the Lowdown

Ten Common College Essay Myths Busted

In the overgrown garden outside my office window, the yellow daylilies I thought could survive an apocalypse were wilting. It was the hottest July day *ever recorded* in Massachusetts, about 1,000 percent humidity (admittedly, my frizzing hair was my barometer).

Melanie arrived in my office, her golden ringlets like curling ribbons bursting from her ponytail. "Ah, you've got air-conditioning," she said to the hardwood floor.

Melanie took up very little space in the same blue velvet chair across from my desk that Tyler had dominated. Unlike Tyler, Melanie bristled with nerves from the moment she entered. She balanced on the edge of the chair, nail-bitten fingers gripping the arms as if bracing for a quick escape.

I said, "It really is a scorcher. Can I bring you a glass of water?"

Melanie reached into her tote bag and extracted a water bottle, held it up to show me she was all set hydration-wise, and clunked it onto the desk between us. Stickers plastered almost every inch of its surface…Lakeview Cross Country, Cuppa Coffee Shop, Ski Utah, Don't Settle, Camp Timberlake, Nature Is My Religion…offering a glimpse into Melanie's juicy inner world that I was eager to help her explore.

"So, do you have any preliminary thoughts about essay topics?" I asked.

Melanie flinched as if I'd slapped her. She white-knuckled the arms of that chair, and can you guess what this girl — who had disclosed via her water bottle that a huge cache of stories brimmed within her — said to me?

Melanie said, "I've heard you should write about something that's totally unique, but I'm just normal and boring."

Have you ever said or thought anything like this about yourself?

All good (always) and no shame (ever) if you, too, have believed any of the common myths swirling around the media, dinner tables, and high school hallways (pretty much everywhere) about the perfect college applicant and legendary college essay. We must bust those falsehoods immediately to free up your brain space for the truth.

Myth 1: I have nothing interesting to say about my normal, boring life.

No one is just normal and boring. I cleared up this misconception with Melanie, and I have the privilege of telling you that you are *special*, in case you were wondering. I know I am right about this because I've never met anyone who wasn't.

Most of us don't recognize our one-of-a-kind qualities, or we take them for granted. Plus, let's face it, society rewards us when we try to blend in. *Unusual* or *eccentric* is not how people describe the Tylers of this world, which makes it hard to wrap our minds around the idea that our differences are *assets*. Remember Tyler's self-effacing Inner Troll voice? If you hear a voice telling you your life is boring and inconsequential, that's what *your* Inner Troll sounds like. Now that you've met this beast, you'll notice it shows up everywhere. Brain Boosters throughout this book will help make sure your Inner Troll's demoralizing words don't linger between your ears for long.

Myth 2: I need to find an epic topic no one has ever written about before.

There are no new topics. I've read essays on every topic from archery to zip-lining. If you're fixated on finding a mind-blowing topic never imagined before, your search will go on forever. Do you care about a topic so much you can't shut up about it? If your topic matters to you, your essay will resonate with readers, even if the topic is not exotic in the least.

Myth 3: I can't write about sports (overdone), any organization connected to religion or politics (too controversial), or...

The rumors floating around — about entire realms of life strictly off-limits for college essay topics — are bogus. You can write about (almost) anything. Use common sense. If you're heavily involved in a political campaign, focus on what you've learned about *yourself* from the experience of organizing or door knocking, not the candidate's politics. It's wonderful if you're deeply invested in community service through your church youth group. Don't avoid writing about impactful, heartfelt involvement just because it's through the church.

Do you suspect someone could be offended? Is it illegal? If so, cross that topic idea off your list (or find a new, less-alarming angle). If you're eager to write about football or political activism or a formative service trip (yes, even that!), you can. It's your *approach* to your topic, not the topic itself, that will influence how fresh or commonplace, fascinating or insulting your essay will turn out.

Myth 4: I need to be funny (or have a sad story) to stand out.

You are enough no matter your personality or what kind of life you've led up to this point. Write a soulful essay if you're an earnest person with a serious story to share. Crack jokes if you're funny. *You being you* will result in the best, most powerful essay. Once you believe what I'm telling you (as Melanie eventually did), you'll find you have much more to say than you thought when you were worrying about who you were not, instead of celebrating who you are.

Myth 5: I need to sell myself in my essay.

Many, many, *many* well-intentioned adults tell students that the college essay is a sales pitch. Please be polite to these loving people while you tune out their misguided advice. Other parts of your college application, including your transcript, activities list (nicknamed the *brag sheet* in admissions offices for a reason), and teacher and counselor recommendations, will do plenty to sell your amazing potential as a college student. Your personal essay is your chance to share who you are as the human being responsible for all the numbers, letter grades, and other data points on your application. It is a glimpse into your soul, not your résumé.

Myth 6: I need to sound smart to impress colleges.

Beware of breaking out the thesaurus to find million-dollar words to make you look smart. You might give an impression like that guy at a casual dance party tossing around words like *leveraged* and *utilized* and looking down his nose at you while explaining the principles of kinesiology. This pretentious (also insecure) look is not the effect we're going for.

No need to dumb down your voice if you're a bookish sort with an extensive vocabulary, but trying to plump up language to impress readers can backfire on the clarity front when it *obfuscates the connotation of your dissertation.* (Do you see what I mean?) Your natural, authentic voice, using the language you really use every day, will draw readers toward you. That's what we want.

Myth 7: I need to cram my entire life story into 650 words.

In this book, we're tackling the personal essay required for the most common college application (aptly named the Common Application), which is used by over one thousand colleges. You can set up a Common Application account for yourself at any time. (There's no time like the present to head to CommonApp .org and commence.) The essay required for the Common Application has a limit of 650 words. On other college applications that require a personal statement read by multiple colleges (such as the Coalition Application), the word count may be different, but all advice included in this book still applies.

One single-spaced typed page is about 650 words. No one can stuff seventeen years into one page. Starting with a topic that's too broad (like a whole life) and attempting the impossible of cramming everything into a single page is a common mistake that dooms an essay before it's even written. I will not let that happen to you. The Magical Shrinking Topic Trick in chapter 4 will help you narrow down your topic until it's so specific only you could write about it. Then the rest of this book will keep you on point, so you'll wind up with a unique essay of a doable scope for 650 words.

Myth 8: I need to choose the right prompt to write a good essay.

You'll encounter seven writing prompts when you open the writing section of the official Common Application (don't stress! It's really just a glorified form like you'd fill out at the doctor's office, only with more writing). We'll analyze those prompts in detail in chapter 3. Prompt 7 on that application asks you to "Share an essay on any topic of your choice," which makes every other prompt *optional*. Prompts exist to help get you started, not to limit you. Whichever prompt you choose will be fine. Or don't use the prompts at all if they make you feel anxious. All good. In chapter 3, you'll encounter multiple methods that will prompt you to conjure exceptional stories.

Myth 9: I need to wait until I feel inspired (and it's 66° Fahrenheit and sunny with 7 mph winds) to start writing.

The first words you spew onto the page are not your college essay. I hope knowing this will remove some pressure to write only when circumstances are perfect. I have a writer friend who pounded out her rough first draft of a feature for *The New York Times Magazine* on an airplane with a restless toddler on her lap *during turbulence*; I kid you not. If she can do that, you can do this (whether you're in your quiet bedroom, a noisy café, or the sky).

No one will ever see those first words you write. They're just the words that will lead you to the next words and the next. So sure, write if you're feeling inspired, but if you're not, write anyway. Inspiration tends to appear while we're tapping on the keyboard, not awaiting the perfect conditions (inside or out).

Myth 10: I'm a bad writer (or not good enough).

Do you think you're a bad or good writer who hates or loves to write? If so, it's time to let go of this black-and-white thinking. A personal essay requires a different kind of writing (creative nonfiction) than the writing required for almost all high school classes (academic), and today you begin with a clean slate.

This may come as a shock, but anyone can write a standout personal essay. All you need to do is show up with a great, can-do attitude, and I promise I'll provide the empowerment tools and clear steps for you to write. I'm honored you've entrusted me as your guide, and I won't let you down.

What Evaluators Are *Really* Looking For (Surprise!)

Welcome to my home office, and please make yourself comfortable in the blue velvet chair (just toss that throw pillow aside like Tyler did if you don't need it). Across the desk, I'm evaluating your application to the college I represent. We'll call it Utopia University. So sorry I didn't dress up for you today. I'm in my sweatpants and slouchy Utopia U sweatshirt, hair piled up in a messy bun, zero makeup or jewelry because I have not left the house today and probably won't until the admissions committee convenes toward the end of February. (It's January now.)

I've been evaluating applications for eight hours straight, lunch at my desk, relying on a cup of tea to perk me up so I can devote my full attention to your essay before I'm rewarded with dinner. I combed through your transcript before you arrived, so I already know your *metrics* — grades, course rigor, test scores (if you submitted them) — and I've seen which activities you've listed as most important. I noticed that your potential major is *undecided* (the most common choice), but based on your transcript (both course selection and grades in the classes you chose), I can wager a guess about what subjects you *might* major in. You look like a qualified applicant for Utopia U! But so do thousands of other students.

I've reached my favorite part of my job, reading your personal essay. I'm hopeful you'll share a story that will suck me into your world for a few minutes, give me insight into the person who produced all those metrics, and maybe even provide a welcome bit of entertainment after all that data analysis. I hope you'll offer a glimpse of your personality and what's truly important to you so I can envision you in the classroom and roaming the campus, contributing to the college's texture, as well as experiencing a life-changing Utopia University education in return. I'm in the business of *finding* students who are a great fit for Utopia U, not weeding out applicants. Surprise!

Do you now see the role your personal essay plays in your application? I very much hope it will transform you from faceless applicant number 5,084 into a three-dimensional person who I feel *connected* to and compelled to fight for in admissions committee after I change out of my sweatpants. Can you see your future reader as a potential ally and champion instead of a critic or adversary?

Despite what you may have heard, college admission evaluators want to like you. We want to support your cause. We hope your successful personal essay will…

- ***sound like you***, in your genuine, conversational voice. If it captures a tiny snippet of what your personality is truly like, it's a success.
- ***engage the reader*** with your story. A good essay wakes up the evaluator, who may have already read thirty-five essays that day, keeps her awake through the middle, and reveals something new about you by the end.
- ***explore a topic important to you*** that you're excited about. Have you ever listened to a friend so fired up it made you feel energized too? Your reader will react in the same way to your enthusiasm.
- ***reflect with some depth*** on the topic, not just *what* you're writing about (soccer), but what you're *really* writing about (your fierce determination), how it serves you, how it can obstruct you when unchecked, and *why* soccer (or camping, or coding, or whatever fascinates you) matters to you.
- ***contain no glaring mistakes*** because those are annoying for the reader and reflect poorly on the writer. But don't worry about mistakes until we reach revisions. A

successful essay proves you're a competent writer who can string together sentences and paragraphs correctly.

Readers are human beings, like you, and the trick to winning them over is to *say what you want to say, not what you think colleges want to hear.*

Fun fact: What you want to say *is* what colleges want to hear.

Do you see now why building up confidence is so important to the success of your essay? You're an *applicant* not a supplicant standing upon the altar of the admissions office with live chickens and pottery and a personal essay to barter. It takes entering a brave, confident headspace to figure out what you want to say, then to write it with authenticity and stand out to an admission reader like me when I'm hungry, tired, and evaluating your application to Utopia University on a frigid winter day. Achieving and sustaining that headspace is our plan.

The Intrepid Applicant (IA) vs. Artificial Intelligence (AI)

Topic: Jill Shulman's Zoom Meeting with Billy
Time: Friday June 29, 01:00 PM Eastern Time (US and Canada)

Join Zoom Meeting
https://us06web.zoom.us/j/84617387552?pwd=JYweFzgvyqqOj8m7Ho8LIuqb7GtLii.1

I could not offer a seat in my blue velvet comfy chair to Billy, who lived across the country from me. He leaned toward his laptop camera, tortoiseshell glasses glinting under his bedroom's overhead light, and confided to me that for a STEM guy like him, the idea of writing a personal essay was especially brutal. He said, "It also seems irrelevant, if you want to know the truth, since I'm applying to colleges for computer science." Then Billy got real. "I was tempted to use AI to write my essay, but I was afraid I'd get caught."

Technology was Billy's love language, and I would never ask a burgeoning computer scientist to avoid experimenting with new technology, as I would never tell you that you should not use spellcheck or autocorrect (AI before large language models) or a calculator (which caused quite a ruckus when introduced into mainstream education in the 1970s) or try any new tech. That would be unrealistic and outright silly if using that tool would help lower your stress. I am all about lowering your stress.

Since you're reading this book, it means you already know using AI to write your essay *for* you is self-sabotage. As Billy understood full well, if caught, it would eliminate you from any college applicant pool before you were even in the running. More importantly, asking AI (or any other new technology available by the time you read this) to write your essay is the kind of cheating that will count against you whether you're caught or not.

Do not fear the chatbots! But don't cheat *yourself* by squandering this opportunity for a deep dive into self-exploration and reflection. Be a badass intrepid applicant (IA) with *confidence* that you are better at sharing your personal story than AI could ever be, as it scrapes the internet for generic stories already told or famously makes them up. You are the world's foremost expert on yourself, and unless you've uploaded your entire memory bank onto the internet, you'll need to look *inside* not outside yourself to find your unique, original story. That's what Billy did before he submitted his one-of-a-kind essay to his first-choice college (and was admitted). You can read Billy's essay in the Appendix.

Leave Jill Shulman's Zoom Meeting with Billy
Time: Friday June 29, 02:00 PM Eastern Time (US and Canada)

BTW, it's not lost on me that videoconferencing technology made my face-to-face meeting with Billy possible in the first place. Respect.

How to Get Out of Your Own Way

Billy (my STEM-oriented student), Melanie (no longer a myth believer), and Tyler (ruler of the school — but not in an arrogant way) all had one thing in common. They each had accumulated a huge stockpile of experiences that had combined to shape the student I met at this juncture of their life, the same crossroads you're facing now. They had *so much* to say, but first they had to face and vanquish their Inner Troll (*bum bum bum bummmmm*).

We all harbor a downer of an Inner Troll, supplier of fear, negativity, and shame, and keeper of an endless list of things we cannot or should not do. Yours will feed you disparaging thoughts such as, *Everything you're writing, thinking, or feeling is wrong and stupid and pointless*. Not one soul can innovate, create, or perform at their personal best under such bullying conditions.

This is the moment for you to recognize and overpower your Inner Troll. Our first exercise might sound a little crazy, but if you have even an inkling of apprehension about writing your essay, just go with it (the exercise, not the apprehension). In merely three minutes, it will restore your sense of humor if, by chance, your obnoxious Inner Troll has stolen laughter along with confidence.

Inner Troll Exorcism

Brain Booster: 3 Minutes

We're not burning sage or calling upon psychics here (though no judgment if that's how you roll). We're using a visualization technique to kick your Inner Troll to the curb.

Instructions

1. **Picture the embodiment of the satanic Inner Troll voice** inside your head. (Mine is a mash-up between a fire-breathing dragon and a slimy green alien.)
2. **Add silly details** to that Inner Troll picture. Some suggestions: a clown nose, floppy dog ears, a frilly princess dress, a purple polka-dot bow tie. (Mine is now 100 percent bubblegum pink and teeters on stilettos.)
3. **Soften its facial expression** until it morphs from aggressive and wicked to submissive and harmless.
4. **Imprison your Inner Troll.** Now that your Inner Troll looks more ridiculous than menacing, march it up, up, up a winding staircase to a remote attic jail (or down, down, down a winding staircase into a dank dungeon). Can you see the jail cell in your mind?
5. **Lock it inside.** Deposit your Inner Troll, clown nose and all, into that prison cell, and padlock the door shut. We're going with the nonviolent solution of ferrying it away, optimally for a life sentence (though realistically, it'll escape every now and then). If you feel a little bit bad about incarcerating it, remember this creature is not human and has tormented you your whole life.
6. **March yourself back down (or up) to the troll-free daylight** so you can start tossing out words without your nasty Inner Troll's ruthless judgments holding you back.

Bonus: This exercise has many practical applications beyond writing, such as quelling nerves before public speaking if envisioning the audience members in their underwear doesn't work.

The Inner Troll's Anthem (aka Myth 11): I have writer's block.

I am not a believer in *writer's block*. That frozen feeling we've all experienced at one time or another is the Inner Troll's voice whispering (or screaming), *Your mind is blank; you have nothing to say*, and so on. If you haven't figured it out by now, your Inner Troll is a no-good lying liar (who is safely locked up now, and good riddance). Your mind is objectively *not* blank. It stows away a lifetime's worth of memories, thoughts, and stories. The only way to begin excavating them is to start writing, so let's get moving on that.

Miracle Cure for Writer's Block

Writing Exercise: 5 Minutes

Using a five-minute timer and a dash of courage, you can conquer your Inner Troll problem whenever it escapes its prison cell and rears its hideous, trash-talking head.

Instructions

1. **Make an appointment** with yourself (now).
2. **Keep it.**
3. **Plant your butt in a chair** in front of a computer (or pen and paper if that's your jam) and wrap your head around the idea that *any* writing, including

what your Inner Troll would consider bad writing, is a victory.

4. **Look at an object in the room.** The first one that catches your eye will do. You know how you can focus your eyes so hard on a single object that everything else around it blurs? Do that.
5. **Start a five-minute timer and type as fast as you can.** Begin writing down every random observation or thought that pops into your head about your object. If your mind wanders onto some other topic, let it, and write about that instead. No self-judgments, even if the string of words spewing out is gobbledygook.
6. **Don't stop typing until the timer dings.** That's your only rule. Stopping will open cracks for self-criticism, fear, and other Inner Troll crap to creep in, and we are done with all that. You might feel stiff at first, but no one will ever see this writing. Keep going.

Ding!

Did it surprise you how many words you could blurt out in less time than it takes to complain about writer's block?

About that timer

At the start of this book, all exercises include a time component, some estimated, some requiring a timer. The purpose of setting a timer while writing is to train yourself to shut out the unwelcome voices of your Inner Troll and Inner Editor while you are busy creating. Plus, it keeps the Brain Booster and Writing Exercises *efficient* for you because you have a life to live beyond your college essay. However, if you try timing your writing for a couple of exercises and the timer makes you anxious, you can skip it thereafter. You do you.

Bye-bye, Inner Troll. Now you're in a great headspace to find your true voice and use it to gush out the words you need. You are ready.

Chapter 2

Think Differently

Prevent the Zombie Apocalypse

You'll unlock a valuable superpower in this chapter: a new way of interacting with the world. Once it's untethered, you'll use this mighty power while you write *and* when you revise your essay, *and* it will enrich all your future writing (bonus!). But with power comes sacrifice. I'm only asking you to make one concession in exchange for a lifetime of superior writing. Ground zero for reaching your potential as a writer (and almost anything else worthwhile), you'll need to turn off your phone.

You cannot merely silence the ringer for this to work. A buzzing in your pocket is as bad as an Inner Troll distraction. It's highly unlikely any real danger will confront you if you don't answer that one text, or if your parent can't reach you for the minutes it will take to complete the exercises in this chapter. (You know in your heart I am right about this.) Please turn off every feature of the device (except your timer if no other timer is available), no matter how much it hurts. If you shut down your phone each time you sit down to write, I promise that you will get used to it (and may come to enjoy the tranquility this one action can bring).

You may already have a hunch that endless, mindless scrolling will transform you into a zombie. I'm sure you've heard before how your phone is manipulating you with addictive algorithms and messing up your brain, but I will leave that issue to the scientists who have confirmed this with multiple studies. I am not your parent confiscating your phone or your teacher approaching you with a locked phone pouch. *I trust you* to turn it off along with all the time-sucking apps on your computer. We're working with an honor code here, as all prospective colleges will expect of you.

If your phone presents a constant temptation (as it does for most of the first world), you can purchase an egg timer at a dollar store and leave your phone in one room while you step into another room to write. Then use this book to awaken your Inner Essayist, who has been dozing while you scroll, waiting for this opportunity to serve you.

Awaken Your Inner Essayist

To build on the positive, confident headspace you earned in chapter 1, I want to put it out there that when it comes to this essay, you have a ton going for you. You're the singular expert on the invisible life teeming inside you where your essay already resides. Your mission is to excavate your stories and ideas and then take dictation when they hit sunlight. One of them will blossom into your college essay. None of this requires natural talent. We are *all* capable of writing a powerful personal essay. Now intensive training begins to make writing *your* college essay easy (and more entertaining than you ever envisioned), starting with three simple steps.

Step 1: Notice what you're noticing.

Fun fact: Everyone, including you, sees the world differently.

When you pay attention to details, what you notice will be different from what I notice, even if we're looking at the same thing at the exact same moment. That's what makes your interactions with the world *personal*.

Case in point, I belong to a community-supported agriculture

(CSA) farm. I pay for a portion of the annual harvest of a hard-working local farmer, Farmer Dan, without doing any gardening myself (important because if I were the gardener, my family would starve). In good years, all the CSA shareholders are flush with produce. In bad years, disease rots Farmer Dan's tomatoes, or bugs consume the lettuce crop, and we shareholders go without (lettuce is mostly water anyway).

Last year was a good year for kale. If I'm being honest (which I will always be with you), I'm not big on kale. But I'm hell-bent on not wasting one leaf of Farmer Dan's labor, so I stood behind the CSA barn on a crisp fall day, overlooking a field with rows of giant kale bouquets, my brain on overdrive formulating recipes to disguise the flavor and texture of that kale. I could concoct a frittata with the fresh eggs sold in the farm shop and add caramelized onions and sharp cheddar cheese to overpower the kale. Or what if I tore those massive leaves into fist-size pieces, seasoned them until unrecognizable, and baked them on a low temperature into kale chips so crunchy and salty they'd transform into a food I might actually enjoy?

My friend Elizabeth appeared beside me and said, "Wow, what a day!" I looked up from the kale field to the foothills of the Berkshire Mountains draped in orange, red, and gold against the blue sky. I had been so consumed with kale-concealing cooking schemes, I was missing the New England fall foliage display people travel miles to see.

Then my husband Mat joined us and said, "I'd love to be a farmer, driving that truck, outside working the soil on a beautiful day like this."

My first thought was that I love my husband and his imagination, but he's the guy who hires the neighborhood teenagers (maybe you?) to mow our lawn, not a guy with a farmer's constitution for hard labor. My second thought was, *What truck?*

Now that Mat had pointed it out, I saw for the first time the green pickup truck parked between the kale field and the mountains performing their colorful leaf show.

As one does in this digital era of constantly sharing (when your phone is not dutifully turned off so you can notice what you're noticing), I snapped a picture of the vista before me and texted it to my mom with the caption "Beautiful day at Brookfield Farm!"

My mom texted back, "Very nice, though that field could use some grooming."

That's my mom. She'd never leave the house without full makeup or perfectly arranged hair, and she'd never have overlooked that splintered wood pile *directly in front of me*, as I had during my kale-obsessed tunnel vision.

My point is that *looking* is not the same as *seeing*. If you look at a farm and note, *It's a farm*, that's a generic observation, something anyone could see. But if you open your eyes wider and notice what you're noticing about the farm, tons of details you've always taken for granted in the world around you will suddenly pop out of the background. This, my new friend, is how you awaken your Inner Essayist.

In the same moment on that same farm, I naturally focused on the food, my nature-loving friend Elizabeth admired the landscape, my husband imagined himself as a farmer, my mom saw the mess, and now you know more personal information about my family (and my friend Elizabeth). College admission evaluators want to know more about you. What does the world look like from your point of view? What do you see in it?

Step 2: Enter full immersion mode.

So much reveals itself when we slow down, turn off our phones, and enter full immersion mode. What you see is a great way to start. But beyond what that farm scene *looked* like on that crisp fall day, I could *hear* the white noise of my fellow shareholders chatting inside the barn behind me and the rumble of a tractor harvesting a distant field. The air *smelled* like composting leaves. I *felt* like one of those kale bunches in the field before me, planted in a community I loved.

Paying attention to all five senses and tapping into our feelings can make everyday experiences one of a kind. Sometimes my husband and I have what we call an *appreciation moment*, and we will stop everything we're doing to silently savor it. Suddenly magic dust sprinkles over a normal scene and makes it special. Go ahead and try it.

Step 3: Write a hot mess, no judgments.

Once you've entered an appreciation moment, I think you know what's coming next. It's time to record in writing what you're noticing. Since you've peeled your eyeballs away from your phone and arrived entirely present on this planet on high alert, you've laid the groundwork to create a virtual reality experience for your reader.

I'm about to ask you to start writing, and keep writing, no matter what spills out, a method called *freewriting*. The Miracle Cure for Writer's Block exercise was a stealth warm-up, so you know how freewriting is done. Most of what *anyone* freewrites at first will surface as a hot mess. But the more words you spray onto the page, the more material you'll have to play with later for this personal essay *and* additional essays you may need to write for individual colleges.

We've established that your college essay demands a different kind of writing than the usual assignments for school, and you've begun training for it. I know it takes courage to write extemporaneously without judging yourself, but trying, even (especially) when it's hard, is a victory when it comes to training for *anything*.

Your Inner Troll is locked in the attic (or basement). Exit all programs on your computer, except your word processor. As with your phone, there is zero need for the internet to distract you. Resist the urge to look up that one thing or take a quick break to check Instagram. Prepare to write some ugly sentences without worrying that anyone will ever see a word of them (they won't). Stay open to surprising yourself, try, fail sometimes, keep writing anyway, and enjoy the ride.

Becoming more comfortable with the uncomfortable is part of the adventure.

Invoke Your Inner Superhero

Brain Booster: 3 Minutes

Instructions

1. **Stand** (literally, stand up) before your computer with a blank page open. Do not fear the inquisition of the blank page.
2. **Strike a pose like a superhero** with perfect posture, feet firmly planted on the floor, fists on hips, and an expression that says, *Do not mess with me. I will prevail.*
3. **Hold that position** until your Inner Superhero takes over your body and mind and you feel your power. (Harvard social psychology professor and bestselling author Dr. Amy Cuddy featured the practical benefits of striking a "power pose" in her book *Presence*. Go for it. No one's watching.)
4. **Now lower your butt into the chair** in front of your computer with the power of the sun radiating from your fingertips, poised to begin typing.

Freewrite Without Fear

Writing Exercise: 10 Minutes

This ten-minute freewriting exercise (no one will ever see) will probably come out in disarray but serves a lofty purpose. If you learn now how to summon your Inner Essayist *at will*, first ideas and then drafts of your college essay will tumble right out.

Instructions

1. **Recall one tiny moment that happened today.** The first moment that pops into your head will work fine. Don't overthink. Do you have one in mind? Use this moment as your topic for this exercise. (If your mind drew a blank, go with brushing your teeth, or taking a bite of breakfast, or petting your dog, or pounding on the bathroom door while your sister hogged the shower, or…Do you have one now?)
2. **Enter full immersion mode.** Close your eyes if it helps. Rewind time to that moment from your very recent past and relive it using all five of your senses. Notice what you're noticing. Can you see, smell, taste, hear, and feel it inside and out? When you can, start your ten-minute timer.
3. **Type fast until that timer ends,** recording every detail you notice. *Go, go, go and do not stop.* Typing at warp speed will ensure that your real, natural voice comes out but your Inner Troll has no room to slip into your head and convince you that whatever you're writing belongs in the garbage (it does not).

Helpful Hints

- **Keep writing through the "stuck" places** (because some of the most interesting stuff comes out right after). If you start to slow down, flip through all your senses again. Wonder why this moment, of all the little moments that occurred today, popped out at you, or why some bristles on the toothbrush are blue while others are white, or whether the energy you expended pounding on the bathroom door made any difference to your sister (and such musings). When you feel tapped out, you can move on to the next moment in your day. Or go off on a random tangent if the wind takes you there. Laugh if a sentence comes out wonky and keep going to the next one. Have some fun!

- **Tough love:** You cannot do this wrong, but if you stop writing for any reason, you must start your timer all over again. This is the only rule, designed to help you lighten up and let go of fear.
- **When the timer dings after ten minutes,** if you're on a roll, feel free to keep typing for as long as you'd like. All writing is good writing, and who knows? Some of it could end up in your college essay.

When you are done for real, shake out your hands and *do not correct or delete a single word*. (If you have perfectionist tendencies, I'm talking to you.) Not a soul will ever read this. Besides, fixing is a job for your Inner Editor (distinct from your banned-for-life Inner Troll), who is not invited to this party until it's time to revise.

Check-in

How did writing without fear go for you? If this was your first stab at freewriting, it might have felt unnatural, liberating, weird, exhilarating, or some new feeling you've never felt before. I validate any feelings you have about your recent writing experience. It's what you *do* with those feelings that matters to your future writing. The more you relinquish any expectation to "get this right," the more freewriting will help you transform your writing from awkward and stiff into a vehicle for your uncensored, unique voice to come out to play. Your Inner Superhero is in charge now to prevent anything from stifling your original voice in Training Boot Camp, up next.

Training Boot Camp

Writing Exercise: 20 Minutes

We're training your mind to abandon inhibitions and permit you to write like no one's watching. I want fearlessness to become second nature for you because confidence of this magnitude will lead to success in essay writing (and life).

Fun fact: No one is ever watching when you write a first draft of anything (besides an in-class essay test, but this is not that).

Fall in. Attennnnnn-tion. Forward march.

Instructions

1. **An overview equation: 4 prompts x 5 minutes each = only 20 minutes of your life.** Now that you know what you're in for, go ahead and set your timer for five minutes.
2. **Start with the first prompt, and write fast,** train-of-thought, no self-judgments (you know the drill from the Freewrite Without Fear exercise you just completed). I challenge you to see how many words you can blurt onto the page before the timer ends.
3. **Repeat steps 1 and 2** for the second, third, and fourth prompts.

Helpful Hints

- **If you're stuck,** tap into your senses (What does it look, smell, sound, taste, and feel like inside and out?), and simply record in writing what you notice.

- **Keep in mind** that during boot camp *all* writing is good writing to build muscle.
- **Feel free to continue** beyond the timer if inspiration pays you a visit while you write.

Prompt 1

Observe an object that's special to you. Describe it in detail. What's so special about it? Keep writing for five minutes until the timer dings.

About face. Reset your timer for five minutes. Change step. March.

Prompt 2

Remember an emotional moment from your past. The first moment of raw emotion that enters your mind will work, whether positive or negative. Relive that moment in writing for the next five minutes.

Mark time. Set your timer for five minutes again. Extend march.

Prompt 3

Reflect on a value that you care about deeply until the timer ends. This one is abstract, so try to articulate answers to some of these questions:

- What is one of your deeply held values?
- How did you first know you had it? Share the *aha* moment.
- What events in your life have reinforced this value for you?
- Why is it so important to you?

One more five-minute timer reset. Left, right, left, right, left.

Prompt 4

Dream big about the best-case-scenario version of where you'll be and what you'll be doing ten years from now. This is an especially fun one IMHO. Step *forward* in time and picture an older, wiser you in a typical moment when you are that person you dream of becoming. Then describe *ideal future you* for five minutes.

You've stretched! Training to think like a personal essayist, complete. Bravery bolstered to try writing differently than you're used to for school papers. The topic safari begins…

Chapter 3

Generate Ideas

The Key to the Topic Hunt

Karina had tried field hockey for one season, dabbled in ceramics, and taken a two-week summer precollege business class at a local university ("My mom signed me up," she told me). Karina confessed at our first meeting, "I've never stuck with an activity very long. I get obsessed with one thing for a while, then move on to the next."

"What's your latest obsession?" I asked.

"Ever since the Winter Olympics, I've been obsessed with watching figure skating videos." Karina's eyebrows rose like question marks. "Is that weird?"

"It does not sound weird to me," I said. "Do you skate?"

"I'm just a beginner, but I make skating videos of the pros. Colleges wouldn't want to hear about that. Do you want to see?"

"Sure," I said, and against every cell in my body warning me to *prevent the zombie apocalypse*, I did not intervene as Karina slipped her phone out of her pocket.

Karina pulled up a video to show me the Russian skater Evgenia Medvedeva spinning and jumping in her Olympic silver medal performance. The skater's dress sparkled as she twirled.

"All those rhinestones are positioned into star constellations," Karina said. She paused the video and spread her thumb and forefinger on the phone screen to zoom in on a cluster. "See the zigzag *W* shape of the beads on her skirt? That's Cassiopeia. I learned about her mythological story when I was, like, twelve and my dad and I made a telescope from a kit."

Aaaaand we were off! "Please tell me more about *that*," I said.

"Oh, that's just stuff I do on my own. I'm into astronomy and mythology, but it's not through the school or anything. None of it counts," Karina said.

But it *did* count, I had the great fortune of telling Karina. *Everything* that's exciting to Karina and to you counts, whether it's organized by the school ("I'm not in any clubs or anything," Karina said) or it's a job ("Well, I've worked at the stationery store in town since middle school"), a hobby ("I'm in the beginner skating class with, like, eight-year-olds, but it's so much fun"), or a fascination ("I can't wait to take an astronomy class in college").

Of course, almost every rule has an exception, and playing video games is one common activity that does not count on your college application. I know many people enjoy the escape video games provide and the connection with other gamers (no judgments here), yet no college wants to risk admitting a student who might isolate in a dorm room playing video games 24-7 instead of contributing to the fabric of the campus. But I digress.

The point I'm trying to make here is not so much *what* to look for when you search for topics, but *where* to look. Karina was looking *outside* herself for an essay topic that she thought others would want to hear about, when the key to finding a unique topic for a truly personal essay was to direct her search *inward*. The same goes for you.

Rewriting a Worn-Out Story

When Karina entered my office, she thought she lacked *stick-to-itiveness*, as her parents called it. She believed she had very little to show for her seventeen years on earth so far, but she had missed the thread.

> Curiosity → copious internet research → watching skating videos → making skating videos → trying skating lessons → recognizing connections between skating, her fascination with astronomy, and storytelling

Once Karina let go of the idea that nothing she'd done was worthy, she felt freed to dig around in the hidden corners of her brain, using the same exercises you'll find in this chapter. Karina had a blast unearthing old memories she'd forgotten all about and thoughts she'd never really articulated before, and then this happened: Karina began to reframe the story she'd told about herself (and others had told about her) for as long as she could remember.

Karina's so-called lack of stick-to-itiveness became curiosity. Her excitement about video editing, figure skating, astronomy, mythology, fantasy stories, and more all counted and began to click together into a form that captured what made Karina tick. By shifting her perspective from cup-half-empty to cup-half-full, Karina could begin reimagining her true story and her own character. Her confidence swelled. You can see Karina's completed essay that oozes confidence in the Appendix.

Your Topic Quest Comes Next

I hope you find as much joy and value on your topic treasure hunt as Karina did. There are moments in the stressful college admissions process that can provide true meaning. Taking a deeper dive inside yourself to discover *what makes you worthy* is one of them.

This chapter includes four exercises that will help you mine the inner recesses of your mind from different angles. At least one of them, if not all four, will lead you to a bonanza of unique topic contenders. We'll do a little weaning away from the timer in this chapter, with *estimated time* each exercise will take you. Continue setting a timer for the estimated time limits if this method has been working for you. Or take as much or as little time as you need to give each exercise meaningful effort without lapsing into overkill.

Caution: Many of the ideas that surface in this chapter will be duds. That's perfectly fine. Who cares about the rubble, when some ideas will glitter with potential? You are the scribe noticing what you're noticing and recording without judgment whatever bubbles to the surface.

If you believe you can, you will.

I *know* you can, and I also predict you'll enjoy rooting around to find out what's lurking inside your brain. Double up on prison security to keep your Inner Troll locked away, use the following Brain Booster to calibrate your headspace to optimum capability, and let the hunt begin.

Swap Excitement for Stress

Brain Booster: Estimated 1 Minute

Fun fact: Anxiety and excitement may seem like opposite emotions, but they are close cousins. Both are aroused emotions (sweaty palms, racing heartbeat), but anxiety can hold you back, while excitement can enhance your performance.

Instructions

When you're feeling nervous, tell yourself, *I am excited!*

Feel the shift from negative energy that obstructs you to positive energy that propels forward motion.

When it comes to writing, once fear and anxiety transform into excitement for the adventure ahead, you can write anything — seriously, *anything* — because you're not afraid to try.

Your positive mindset is your strongest weapon to crush this essay and countless other challenges in your life.

Crack the Application Code

The essay instructions and prompts on the Common Application can help more than haunt you if you know where to look. If those that appear right now on the Common Application look different than the ones I've examined below, don't worry. They can change from year to year, but not that much, and all the advice ahead still applies.

Let's Analyze the Instructions

Contrary to popular belief, colleges want to help you speak your truth, not trip you up. It's no big mystery what readers hope to see; it's all embedded in the personal essay instructions.

> The essay demonstrates your ability to write clearly and concisely on a selected topic and helps you distinguish yourself in your own voice. What do you want the readers of your application to know about you apart from courses, grades, and test scores? Choose the option that best helps you answer that question and write an essay of no more than 650 words, using the prompt to inspire and structure your response. Remember: 650 words is your limit, not your goal. Use the full range if you need it, but don't feel obligated to do so. (The application won't accept a response shorter than 250 words.)

When we break down these instructions into their component parts, you'll see how they can guide you in the right direction.

"The essay demonstrates your ability to write clearly and concisely…"

Sure, but not on the first try! Start by plopping words onto the page. Later, you'll revise to make sure your essay is clear and concise.

"...on a selected topic..."

There are seven official prompts (which we will analyze in the next section). Do not stress if none of them inspires you, because the seventh gives you the opportunity to write about any topic at all, making all the other prompts *optional.*

"...and helps you distinguish yourself in your own voice."

Your authentic, natural, conversational voice — the one that automatically appears when you write without fear — distinguishes you from everyone else.

"What do you want the readers of your application to know about you..."

This is what colleges hope to learn when they read your essay. It's not a secret. I repeat, what you want to say is what they want to hear, as stated explicitly in the instructions. I did not make this up.

"...apart from courses, grades, and test scores?"

Colleges do not want a recap of data they've already studied. They want to meet the human being behind that data.

"Choose the option that best helps you answer that question and write an essay of no more than 650 words, using the prompt to inspire..."

That number, 650 words (about one single-spaced page), is the *maximum* word count for your essay, not the requirement. If it's one word over, the Common Application powers that be will lop the 651st word right off.

"...and structure your response."

The prompts can help guide how you organize your essay. I'll show you how below.

"Remember: 650 words is your limit, not your goal."

It's a favorite Inner Troll pastime to worry about editing stuff before you have even written anything to edit. Don't obsess over word count! But do keep in mind, when exploring topics, that no one can fit their entire life story into only 650 words.

"Use the full range if you need it, but don't feel obligated to do so. (The application won't accept a response shorter than 250 words.)"

Some students don't need all the words allotted by the Common Application to share their story. Check out Max's essay in the Appendix of this book for a successful essay shorter than 650 words.

Tips for Using the Prompts for Your Benefit

Fun fact: Which prompt you choose doesn't matter.

PROMPT (verb): to move to action

— Merriam-Webster Dictionary

The prompts on the Common Application are broad. They're meant to nudge you across the threshold and into your inner world, where you can roam in whatever direction you fancy. However, prompts have the opposite effect on some students, who stare at the official prompts on the official application and spiral into a panic (*If I don't choose the right prompt, I'm going to tank this essay and never get into a good college or become a successful, happy person*). Then they freeze with fear, as in a nightmare.

No wonder their mind goes blank as their Inner Troll spews misinformation (as usual). If this happens to you when you look at essay prompts, march your Inner Troll (which sometimes escapes its confines) back to its jail cell. Add a chain to the padlock and yell, "I am excited!" over your Inner Troll's baseless doomsaying. The questions hold the answers, so we'll use the prompts on the Common Application (as they appear at the time of this writing) in the way they were intended, to jiggle your mind so ideas topple out.

Prompt 1

> Some students have a background, identity, interest, or talent that is so meaningful they believe their application would be incomplete without it. If this sounds like you, then please share your story.

"Some students have a *background*, *identity*, *interest*, or *talent*..."

The Common Application hopes one of these four key words in italics will prompt you to think of a fabulous idea. If not, you can use the key words to brainstorm later.

A means "pick *one*." Narrowing your focus, no matter what topic you choose, will prevent you from starting with a topic that's too broad, one of the most common mistakes students make that leads to a generic essay.

"...that is so meaningful they believe their application would be incomplete without it."

If it's meaningful to you, and you write from your heart, it will be meaningful to the reader, who will read with theirs. That's the way good writing works.

"If this sounds like you, then please share your story."

Some students think this prompt only applies to students with extraordinary circumstances, such as founders of Fortune 500 companies, Olympic gold medalists, or those with an origin story of extreme heartbreak and survival. But *everyone* has a background, interest, or talent central to their identity. What's yours? This prompt is so broad and general that it loosely translates to "write about a topic of your choice." If you feel liberated knowing that, wonderful! If it overwhelms you, let's scamper right along to the next prompt.

Prompt 2

> The lessons we take from obstacles we encounter can be fundamental to later success. Recount a time when you faced a challenge, setback, or failure. How did it affect you, and what did you learn from the experience?

"The *lessons* we take from *obstacles* we encounter can be fundamental to *later success*."

This first sentence gives you the pertinent information. Colleges are more interested in the lessons we take from obstacles than the obstacles themselves. But it's a lead-in to the question. It asks nothing of you. Use the key words *obstacles*, *lessons*, and *later success* to start your thought juices flowing. Then read on to the next sentence in pursuit of the actual question colleges hope you'll answer.

"Recount *a time*…"

Once more with feeling: *A time* means "pick *one* time." The prompt aims to help you narrow down your topic to avoid a generic response that doesn't do you justice and leads to a boring read.

"…when you faced a *challenge*, *setback*, or *failure*."

You can use these key words to brainstorm ideas — perhaps not your finest moments, but humility can endear people to you in life as well as personal essays.

"How did it affect you, and *what did you learn* from the experience?"

This sentence finally reveals the question for you to answer, all the way at the end of the prompt. This prompt does not want you to dwell on how you failed. It asks you to adopt a positive attitude and share what happened *after* you hit a snag, how you transformed a potential failure into a lesson learned.

Prompt 3

> Reflect on a time when you questioned or challenged a belief or idea. What prompted your thinking? What was the outcome?

"Reflect on *a time*…"

Need I repeat, *pick one* time? Trying to include multiple times is a common student mistake that results in a summary rather than a personal story.

"…when you *questioned* or *challenged* a *belief* or *idea.*"

The key words *belief* and *idea* are included for you to mull over. If you feel passionate about a fervent belief or idea, by all means write about it. Just make sure to focus your essay on the pivotal moment when you *questioned* or *challenged* it, followed by the way you acted and reflected upon the belief or idea, not a long explanation of the belief or idea itself.

"What *prompted* your thinking?"

This is one of those places where the Common App is trying to provide help with structuring your essay. Try starting your essay with your answer to this question.

"What was the *outcome*?"

And you can try ending your essay with the answer to this question.

Prompt 4

> Reflect on something that someone has done for you that has made you happy or thankful in a surprising way. How has this gratitude affected or motivated you?

"Reflect on something that someone..."

Something = one thing. Someone = one person.

"...has done for you that has made you happy or thankful in a surprising way."

The Common Application added this prompt during the pandemic in response to anxiety and depression rates spiking. They hope to help you tilt toward positive thinking.

"How has this *gratitude* affected or motivated you?"

Gratitude can be a powerful change agent. Take this opportunity for an *appreciation moment*, regardless of whether you choose this prompt for your essay. Look around you and reflect on everything you have and the people who love you. You won't regret it.

Prompt 5

> Discuss an accomplishment, event, or realization that sparked a period of personal growth and a new understanding of yourself or others.

"Discuss an *accomplishment*, *event*, or *realization*..."

I'm sure you've had many, but *pick one* of these key words to chew on.

"...that sparked a period of *personal growth* and a new understanding of yourself or others."

Significant moments in our lives change us. But this is not asking you to write a story about a significant accomplishment, event, or realization. It's asking you to write about *the aftermath* of that accomplishment, event, or realization. Use most of your essay space to share how you've grown and changed since it happened.

Prompt 6

> Describe a topic, idea, or concept you find so engaging that it makes you lose all track of time. Why does it captivate you? What or who do you turn to when you want to learn more?

"Describe a *topic*, *idea*, or *concept* you find so engaging that it makes you lose all track of time."

This prompt invites you to write about what you love, love, *love*, the thing you talk about constantly, the thing that leads you down a Reddit rabbit hole, like Karina's figure skating video obsession. Enjoy!

"*Why* does it captivate you?"

Share what's so amazing about your passion, and the reader will feel your positive energy.

"*What* or *who* do you turn to when you want to learn more?"

Give that person or resource credit, but avoid wandering off into an essay about *them*. Remember, this is an essay about *you*.

Prompt 7

> Share an essay on any topic of your choice. It can be one you've already written, one that responds to a different prompt, or one of your own design.

"Share an essay on *any topic* of your choice."

Here it is, the prompt that says *all the other prompts are optional*.

"It can be one you've already written..."

But *not an academic paper* you've written for school (though a college may request one in another part of the application). This is a different kind of essay.

"...one that responds to a different prompt, or one of your own design."

Go nuts if you're feeling creative!

The upshot of what analyzing the prompts can teach us

- ***Contemplate key words*** to help you find a topic.
- ***Pick one*** (time, person, thing, etc.) to narrow your focus for a more personal approach.
- ***Write about what's meaningful*** to you.
- ***Include why*** your topic is meaningful to you.
- ***Share growth*** from an event or obstacle you experienced.
- ***The question often appears at the end*** of a multisentence prompt.
- ***You are the real topic*** of this essay, regardless of which prompt you choose.
- ***You can write about anything you want.*** If none of the Common Application's prompts calls out to you, move on.

Idea Dump

Writing Exercise: Estimated 5 Minutes

Instructions

Jot down your topic ideas so far, so you'll have a list all in one place.

1. **Record ideas unearthed by prompts** on the Common Application.
2. **Add ideas sparked by freewriting** you did in chapters 1 and 2.
3. **Add ideas you already had** before you picked up this book.

If no ideas have come to mind yet, no need to fret. Continue to the next exercise.

House of Mirrors Questionnaire

Writing Exercise: Estimated 25 Minutes

Instructions

Type fast, freewriting responses to each of the fifty questions below. Enjoy winding through the labyrinth of topic ideas already inside you!

Helpful Hints

- **Be real** and unleash your natural voice, like you did when you wrote without fear. Ignore grammar and "getting it right" (there is no right or wrong). We're digging for *content*, not correctness.
- **I'm estimating it will take you about thirty seconds per question** if you blurt a couple of train-of-thought sentences and have some fun with your answers. If you overthink and treat this like a term paper, this exercise will take days (which is not the assignment or expectation).

Topic-Generating Questions

1. What do you honestly spend most of your time doing outside of the classroom, and why?

2. What do you talk about so much that it might drive your family or friends crazy?
3. What is the hardest and/or best part about being you?
4. What's something unusual about your daily routine?
5. What memory do you have of a special place?
6. What made you so enraged that your face turned bright red and cartoon steam burst out of your ears (not literally, of course, but with that intensity of anger)?
7. What do you love that other people might find weird?
8. What was one of your proudest moments? What did you learn from it?
9. What would make you a better person?
10. What's the first smell that pops into your mind? What does that smell remind you of?
11. What's your *spirit animal* and why?
12. What's something most people do not understand about you?
13. What experience still triggers high emotion (positive or negative) when you think about it?
14. What's your favorite food, and why do you love it so much?
15. When did nature bring you down or lift your spirits?
16. What's amazing about your favorite academic subject?
17. What's your big dream, the thing you'd do if you could accomplish anything?
18. What memory is triggered by a specific sound?
19. What would be the cover image on your first solo album or book jacket?
20. When did you speak up, and what happened when you did?
21. What was a big transition in your life when everything changed for you?
22. What or who has inspired you?

23. When did you go above and beyond to help?
24. How has gratitude for something someone else did for you affected or motivated you?
25. What happened that was hilarious?
26. What happened that made you cry (or very sad)?
27. When did you change your mind?
28. Who do you love most and why?
29. What object holds special meaning for you and why?
30. What family experience had an impact on you?
31. What's a memorable moment you had with a friend?
32. What's your greatest hope for your future?
33. What secret have you been holding inside?
34. What's a core value that matters to you so much you've fought for it (or would fight for it)?
35. Where do you fit in best?
36. What did you do to overcome a big challenge or obstacle you have faced?
37. What is the same or different between the way your family or friends would describe you versus the way you'd describe yourself?
38. What important decision did you make?
39. What weakness have you been working on (or do you feel like you should be working on)?
40. What activity or topic captivates you so much you lose track of time?
41. What's something interesting about your background?
42. What would you say or do differently if you had a do-over?
43. What have you created?
44. What or who is captured in a photograph you like?
45. What idea did you hear or read that resonates for you?
46. How did you push through a situation that tested your limits?

47. What's your superpower?
48. What are you noticing right now?
49. What would you like people to know about you?
50. What theme(s) have come up while answering these questions?

Brain Hurricane

Writing Exercise: 10 Minutes

Brainstorming is freewriting in list form. Some people enjoy writing train-of-thought lists in response to single words better than they like answering questions with full sentences as you did in that last exercise. So let's give brainstorming a try to stir up more memories and ideas for this essay and additional essays you may need to write down the road.

Instructions

1. **Flick the switch in your head to game mode.** We're brainstorming, but at cyclone velocity, trying to beat the clock (it's more fun if you use a timer on this one).
2. **Start a ten-minute timer and write as fast as you can,** listing moments, events, and memories that pop into your head. Use the "words for inspiration" below to keep the flow going. I challenge you to see how many thoughts you can capture on the page before time runs out.

Helpful Hint

- **Continue to type fast** even if you need to type *No ideas, nothing, nada* until the next word for inspiration sparks your next idea to appear (trust that it will). That way, you'll leave no cracks for your Inner Troll to sneak in and undermine you.

- **Feel free to carry on** listing ideas still surfacing after the timer dings.

Words for Inspiration

- Obsessions
- Events
- Family
- Friends
- Holidays
- School (go backward from now to kindergarten)
- Work
- Play
- Activities
- Food
- Spring/summer/winter/fall

Breathing Lessons

Brain Booster: Estimated 2 Minutes

Let's slow down your brain after that whirlwind of activity. Take a few long, deep, cleansing breaths, and focus all your energy on the air expanding inside you and releasing.

Instructions

Inhale. Exhale. Inhale. Exhale. Inhale. Exhale.

Repeat until you feel relaxed and ready for a deep dive into your inner sanctum in the next exercise (but stop before you hyperventilate).

Down the Reflection Rabbit Hole

Writing Exercise: Estimated 10 Minutes

Reflection elevates a good personal essay to a great one, and producing a great personal essay is our plan. I've estimated about one minute per question, but please take your time plunging deeper inside yourself.

Instructions

Answer the following questions, knowing full well that your responses could be different today than they will be tomorrow (or next week or next year or in ten years), and that's okay.

1. What motivates you every day?
2. What are your most sacred values?
3. What or who has influenced what you value?
4. Who are you at this moment in time?
5. How have you changed and grown into someone different from who you used to be?
6. What makes you different from your classmates, friends, family, or other people?
7. What truly makes you sparkle?
8. What are your dreams and goals for your future?
9. Who do you want to become?
10. How will going to college help you academically, socially, and emotionally to become the person you hope to be?

Optional interview: If you come up short answering these big questions (or if you're curious), interview someone close to you about how they see you. *Regard their answers as one opinion, not the truth.* You and you alone can write (or re-write) your own story.

Interview Questions

1. How would you describe me to someone who doesn't know me?
2. What qualities make you love me (or want to be my friend)?
3. What's a fun or meaningful memory you have of me?
4. After thinking about it, do you still love me (or want to be my friend)?

Just kidding on this last one; *of course* they love you (and want to be your friend) even more after they've thought about it.

Idea gold mine gathered! It's time to get choosy…

Chapter 4

Choose a Unique Topic

Decision-Making 101

The greatest mistake you can make in life is to be continually fearing that you'll make one

— Elbert Hubbard

You deserve a round of applause for advancing from *nothing* to collecting a gold mine of ideas! Now we search for the shiny nuggets hidden in the gravel. By the end of the topic tournament in this chapter, you'll have your essay topic. (Crazy, right?) This will require you to make a series of decisions, and if you have trouble making decisions when it counts, you are not alone. My student Darius had generated dozens of ideas, as you have, and indecisiveness kicked in when the time came to narrow them down.

"I like all my ideas," Darius said. "What if I choose wrong?"

As a refresher from way back in chapter 1, your *approach* to your topic, not the topic itself, will make your essay personal and memorable. That means no pressure on Darius (or on you) to find an end-all-be-all topic. Most of the ideas you cooked up in chapter 3 could work as the seed for your essay.

On the opposite end of the spectrum, Darius's twin sister, Jasmine, told me, "I *hate* all my ideas. I'll keep thinking of more until I find the right one."

Once the spigot opens, the flow of ideas can go on *forever*, so I needed to tell Jasmine there's no single right idea. Enough was enough.

Even siblings who share a birthday and half their DNA can be soooo different, yet my advice was the same for both Darius and Jasmine: *Ditch the idea of perfect.*

I managed to convince the twins they had better things to do with their time than to squander it agonizing over essay topics. The same applies to you. Efficient decision-making tips are coming right up.

Tip 1: Keep this decision in perspective.

Perspective alone is a great stressbuster that can help you complete tasks and have more fun while doing them. Your essay is one piece of your multipage college application. Within the scheme of your life, choosing your college essay topic is a tiny decision. If you know you're a person who treats every decision as if your life depended on it, please set yourself a time limit for exercises all the way through this book.

Tip 2: When in doubt, trust your gut.

To avoid wasting time and energy overthinking decisions, *stop judging them*. A decision by itself is not good or bad. It's an action that keeps us moving forward. But once our Inner Troll places a value judgment on a decision, the second-guessing and overthinking begin. Confidence in your own instincts will help you continue your forward momentum and will result in a better essay than ruminating over every little thing.

Tip 3: Enthusiasm is contagious in writing (as in life).

Topics that surprise, intrigue, or otherwise capture *your* attention are what you're looking for as you narrow down your topic list step-by-step in this chapter. If *you* feel fired up, your reader will feel that too. Your excitement about the topic can help guide the series of little decisions you'll make leading to your ultimate topic choice.

Mother Lode Master List

Writing Exercise: Estimated 10 Minutes

Instructions

Open a fresh document and paste into it every idea from your chapter 3 idea-generating exercises:

1. Idea Dump
2. House of Mirrors
3. Brain Hurricane
4. Down the Reflection Rabbit Hole

You have a big, honking list ready for the topic-determining tournament ahead. Before you discard a single idea, please understand that most could work. But some ideas will blend into the dirt pile you dug up, while others will twinkle like gems when you revisit them. Trust your gut, amp up your enthusiasm, and here comes a little help with keeping perspective as you make decisions.

What If It's Not a Problem?

Brain Booster: Estimated 2 Minutes

Instructions

If you find yourself spiraling about any decision, ask yourself, *What if it's not a problem?*

Cheryl Vigder Brause, a mindfulness instructor and cofounder of Pause to be Present, taught me this quick, easy way to relieve stress and gain perspective if we start to freak out. (Most of our worries are not about a real problem.)

The tournament begins!

First Elimination Round

Writing Exercise: Estimated 10 Minutes

The best topics are the ones most meaningful to you that you're most excited to write about. The worst topics are the ones you think you *should* write about because you're trying to guess what college admission officers will like.

Instructions

1. **Look at all the ideas you generated in chapter 3** (raucous applause for your effort). If that long Mother Lode Master List overwhelms you at first glance, say, "I am excited!" because wow, look what you did.
2. **Choose ten to twenty topic ideas from that list** that call out to you *today*. Highlight no fewer than ten and no more than twenty. No second-guessing. Trust your gut and go with your first impressions.
3. **Make a new list** that includes only those ten to twenty highlighted topics.
4. **Now move on.** No looking back.

See, narrowing down your list was a cinch, correct? Onward.

Second Elimination Round

Writing Exercise: Estimated 5 Minutes

Remember that your topic decisions are not right or wrong. A decision is an action to keep your momentum moving forward, and forward momentum is your best friend when it comes to efficiency.

Instructions

Choose four top topic ideas from your list of ten to twenty.

I know you could have chosen different topic ideas yesterday, or alternative ones may attract you tomorrow, or you could spend copious time deliberating. Ignore your Inner Troll's mantra of "Could have, would have, should have." Seize the moment, and just do it. Then stick with these four topics that you're most excited to explore here and now.

The Magical Shrinking Topic Trick

Congratulations! You have made it to the quarterfinals (woot, woot). You've narrowed down your topic list to four ideas. I'll bet pursuing any of them would work out fine, as long as they're not too broad. Starting with a topic that's too broad will doom an essay to emerge generic and blend into the applicant pool. So we're taking a brief time-out from decision-making to narrow the *scope* of your quarterfinalist topics to make sure your approach to each is so specific only you could write about any of them.

Do you remember in chapter 3 when we analyzed the Common Application prompts? I pointed out ad nauseam that when you see the word *a* in a prompt it directs you to *pick one*. That is the Common Application's way of helping you make choices to shrink a topic until it's as distinctive as you are.

Cassidy's Shrinking Topic

I introduce you to my student Cassidy to demonstrate the Magical Shrinking Topic Trick in action. From my first meeting with her, it became clear Cassidy loved, loved, *loved* visual art. Cassidy was leaning toward writing her essay about art as she entered the quarterfinals of her topic tournament.

But anyone who loves to draw, paint, sculpt, or view artwork at a museum can say she loves art. Cassidy was headed toward a generic essay — the likes of which millions of students could write — until the Magical Shrinking Topic Trick helped her pick the one visual art form she loved the most. No matter that sophomore year she'd spent significant time on charcoal drawing, or that she'd registered for a ceramics class for senior year. At the moment we met, painting was Cassidy's preferred artistic medium.

Narrowing her topic from *all* art to painting was a great start for Cassidy, but painting was still too broad. Millions of people love to create or admire all sorts of paintings. Cassidy needed to pick one style of painting she loved to shrink her topic further. She had painted still life, landscape, and abstract paintings, but she was a people person who loved painting portraits the most.

Portrait painting was still too broad a topic for a 650-word essay. Cassidy couldn't write about all the portraits she'd ever painted, so she brainstormed *specific* portraits she'd created to pick one and shrink her topic again. You can brainstorm specifics for your topic in your head if you'd like. However, Cassidy enjoyed timed writing, so she set a timer for five minutes and brainstormed on the page a list of portraits she'd painted. Here's an excerpt from her brainstorming session:

- Acrylic self-portrait painted in junior year art class
- Acrylic of Amy with still life
- Self-portrait gouache in seventh grade (too long ago)
- Watercolor of Rolo as a puppy
- That oil family portrait Mom loves
- Holiday watercolor portrait gifts for Mel, Jonathan, Sandy
- Oil painting of Mika for the Memory Project

Boom!

Cassidy had never met Mika, a little girl who lived in an orphanage in Kenya. But Cassidy told me she felt like she knew Mika after spending so many hours studying her face to paint her portrait as a gift for the Memory Project, a school service club in which Cassidy was deeply invested. Landing on this one very specific painting combined Cassidy's love for art *and* the Memory Project initiative, achieving *the two most important criteria for a standout personal essay topic*:

1. Only Cassidy could write about this.
2. The thought of writing about it excited her.

Plus, Cassidy's topic of choice embraced one of her finest qualities: her empathy. You can read Cassidy's successful personal essay, so specific that only she could have written it, in the Appendix.

Applying the Magical Shrinking Topic Trick to Your Writing

The next exercise is for narrowing down only the topic ideas that need tweaking, not messing with a good thing for those that already seem specific enough and fine to you as they are. The upshot of the Magical Shrinking Topic Trick: Use the *pick one* method like Cassidy did, and continue to narrow down your idea until you've landed on a topic so specific that only you could write about it, and the thought of writing about it excites you.

You'd think you'd have more to say about a broader topic, but not so. You'll see that the narrower your topic, the more details to write about, yet another cool (some might say magical) thing about writing. In the next exercise, you'll have a chance to use the Magical Shrinking Topic Trick to narrow down each of your quarterfinalist topics if you need to. Or you can file this trick away because it will come in handy again later in the book.

Stealth weapon locked and loaded. Back to making decisions in the quarterfinals.

Shrink It!

Writing Exercise: Estimated 10 Minutes

Let's give all four of your quarterfinalists a fighting chance for success by narrowing down each one into a viable topic for a short personal essay (650 words is short).

Instructions

Use the Magical Shrinking Topic Trick to narrow down the scope of your quarterfinalist topics and adjust them, as needed.

Helpful Hints

- **If you suspect a topic is too broad,** repeatedly pick one event, place, moment in time, etc., until you've landed on a topic so specific that only you could write about it and the thought of writing about it excites you.
- **If you set your timer for ten minutes** to fiddle with whichever topics need tightening, you won't have time to waste overthinking. This is *not* your last opportunity for tweaking.

Topic-Testing Quarterfinals

Writing Exercise: 20 Minutes

You know how to disempower your Inner Troll (add a very unscary clown nose and tutu). You know how to conjure your Inner Essayist (enter full immersion mode, notice what you're noticing, and record it in writing). Now comes the fun part as we return to no-strings-attached freewriting.

Instructions

1. **Set your timer for five minutes and write as fast as you can** on the first of your four quarterfinalist topics until the timer runs out. No stopping, no overthinking, no judging, no corrections. Play on the page and enjoy exploring.
2. **Then reset your timer and repeat step one again** (and again and again) for the other three topics still in the running (twenty minutes total).

Helpful Hints

- **Use all five senses** (what you see, smell, hear, taste, and feel inside and outside your body). Notice what you're noticing and record the details.
- **Consider why you care about this topic.** Tunnel into a reflection rabbit hole if you have time.
- **Embrace the adventure.** Remind yourself no one will ever see this freewriting, so it's zero-stakes, and you are *excited* to discover what will spring up next.

Championship Playoff Quiz

Writing Exercise: Estimated 10 Minutes

You have nailed decision-making so far and made it to the playoffs. Hooray! Keep that decisiveness going for the win.

Instructions

Check the box beside all statements that are true for each of your quarterfinalist topics. Then tally up your checkmarks to reveal a winner.

Topic 1	Topic 2	Topic 3	Topic 4	
❑	❑	❑	❑	I enjoyed freewriting about this topic and had plenty to say.
❑	❑	❑	❑	I felt honest and authentically myself while freewriting about this topic.
❑	❑	❑	❑	I spend significant time in my life doing or thinking about this topic.
❑	❑	❑	❑	This topic fits my personality as it is now.
❑	❑	❑	❑	This topic shows how I've grown over time.
❑	❑	❑	❑	This topic is meaningful to me.
❑	❑	❑	❑	I'm the central character in my freewriting about this topic.
❑	❑	❑	❑	This topic reveals something about me that's different from my peers.
❑	❑	❑	❑	This topic relates (either directly or peripherally) to something I want to study, participate in, or continue pursuing in some way while in college.
❑	❑	❑	❑	My approach to this topic is unlikely to appear offensive or concerning to someone who doesn't know me.
❑	❑	❑	❑	This topic highlights something positive about me that I want colleges to know.
❑	❑	❑	❑	I'm curious about this topic and excited to explore it further.
❑	❑	❑	❑	My gut tells me this is the best topic for me.

Totals: Topic 1 _____ Topic 2 _____ Topic 3 _____ Topic 4 _____

Did one of your topics clearly stand out? If so, *the winning topic is ________!* If not, this calls for a tiebreaker.

Sudden-Death Overtime

Writing Exercise: Estimated 5 Minutes

This is not a life-or-death decision (no matter how desperately your Inner Troll tries to convince you otherwise). Readers want to hear your voice. Your topic is a *portal* into your inner world that no one can access without you showing them the way. So let's show them the way!

Instructions

Use the following tiebreaker questions to make your decision.

- **Which topic was most fun to write about?** The most interesting and inspiring topic to *you* will resonate best with your reader.
- **Can you rule out a topic that takes place in the distant past?** That topic may be too difficult to remember clearly, or perhaps it reflects you at a much younger age, not as you are now.
- **Can you rule out a topic that could prove controversial?** If your approach to the topic sticks to stories about you, you're probably okay. If your approach to the topic could feel to readers like you're teaching or preaching about a belief you hold dear, this may be a topic to eliminate now.
- **Can you find a connection between the topics tied for the lead?** If so, there could be a theme emerging. Pick one of these topics to begin your essay, and in chapter 5 I'll show you how to plan your essay around a theme.
- **Do you like your finalists equally?** The probability is high that all four of your quarterfinalist ideas could work. At this juncture, pick one and go with it. The runner(s)-up could become examples in the middle of your essay or prove useful in another part of your college application.

- **Do you need a second opinion?** If your Inner Troll's fearmongering voice is what's driving you to seek outside help, plug your ears. However, if you're 100 percent sure hearing someone else's opinion won't end up deflating your enthusiasm, choose a trustworthy person to vet your topic options. If another's input will truly help you feel more confident moving forward, go for it. But you *must* move forward.

You have a winning topic idea! Now we scheme…

Part II

DRAFT 1 — THE HOT MESS (WITH POTENTIAL FOR GREATNESS)

Chapter 5

Hatch a Plan

Are You a Planner or (Seat-of-the) Pantser?

"I have an outline for my college essay. What do you think?" my student Priya asked at our first meeting.

Priya handed me her multipage outline, and, my friend, that outline included *Roman numerals* and *footnotes*. Priya had spent more time creating a perfect outline for an essay she never ended up writing than she spent writing the essay that helped bump her off the waitlist into her top-choice college.

Priya's completed essay is included in the Appendix, born from a plan I'll walk you through in this chapter. You have a topic you're excited about for an essay only you can write. Well done, you. Please don't waste time second-guessing yourself because the topic you chose in the last chapter is just a starting point for exploring the *real* topic of your essay (you).

Do You Tilt Toward Planning or Pantsing?

Some people are planners, while others are (seat-of-the) pantsers. If you are that person who always knows where you're going and maps out a detailed itinerary, you are a planner like Priya. If you enjoy wandering the back roads to see where they lead, you're a pantser. Planning and pantsing are both totally fine. Identify yourself *without judgment*. Most of us have elements of both, but you know which way you lean.

The Beauty and the Beast of Planning

You'll see articles and whole books that include charts, spreadsheets, worksheets, and twelve-step processes to structure your essay before you write, as if you're planning a military operation (which you are not). This is not that book.

No shame for being who you are if you're a planner. Planning and pantsing are both good *in moderation*. Extremes, as with anything, are not optimal. I'm an advocate of planning, but *overplanning is a form of procrastination* and a favorite Inner Troll pastime that distracts you from doing the thing you're planning to do (in this case, writing an essay). If you've felt the urge to organize your desk or clean out your closet before you plot an expansive outline for a paper, you know exactly what I mean. If you're prone to overplanning, like Priya, march your slippery Inner Troll back to its jail cell for the sake of efficiency *and* a better essay.

I know how much you love to organize if you're a planner. I'll provide tools in this chapter for you to plan enough to calm your methodical mind without overkill. If you're a structure and organization fanatic (and you really need a fix), you can flip ahead to chapter 8, where most of your essay's shaping and structuring will happen *after* you write your first draft, but please don't linger there. We have writing to do first.

The Beauty and the Beast of Pantsing

Pantsers enjoy the adventure of discovery along the way as they write, a boon for creativity! But *extreme pantser procrastination* can present in the form of putting off writing until the last minute, then sitting down to wing it the day (or hour) before the paper (or college application) is due.

Extreme pantsers ride the wave of an adrenaline rush by racing a deadline, which doesn't leave them time for much (if any) revision, a cornerstone of a solid personal essay. Pantsing your way through a first draft can be a fun and fruitful adventure, but submitting that first draft without revising it would come at a cost. Are you a pantser whose last-minute papers have worked out fine so far? If so, I'm thrilled you picked up this book to enter the brave new world of revision because once you start college, the coasting is over.

Why You Can Choose Whether or Not to Use a Timer Now

Planners notoriously overdo it. They'll spend three hours researching background information or three days filling out a questionnaire intended to take under an hour. I've been there and done that. Timed exercises help planners stay efficient.

Pantsers notoriously underdo it. They'll dash off a few words rather than slowing down to notice what they're noticing now or think through revisions later. Timed exercises help them raise their own expectations of what's possible for them to achieve.

By now you know whether timing your writing exercises is helpful for you. If you find it stressful or unnecessary, set the timer aside and take your own sweet time. If time boundaries help you with efficiency or motivate you to raise the bar on effort, keep on timing. In this chapter and the next one, I'll continue to provide time estimates. In parts III and IV, the time guidelines will disappear. As a general rule moving forward, you can set your timer for *thirty minutes for writing exercises and five minutes for Brain Boosters.*

A Parachute Plan for Planners and Pantsers Alike

In this chapter, you'll make an appropriately *rough outline* for your *rough essay draft*. We're talking about sketching out a place to begin, a couple of touchpoints to hit in the middle, a place to end, and that is all. I call it a *Parachute Plan* because you'll sew together a safety net as backup in case you float adrift at any point while you write.

If you're a planner, this method will provide security as you write your essay draft, but it won't become a straitjacket. If you're a pantser, you'll have a place to start and an ending to write toward with liberty to meander in between. Writing rarely goes exactly according to plan anyway, so no need to work yourself up creating an intricate outline for your first essay draft.

Common Essay Structures Oversimplified

A *narrative* structure means you start at the beginning, continue your story in chronological order (what happened first, next, after that, and so on), and end where it ends. Some narratives share big stories about events spanning lots of time, such as an activity you've participated in your whole life. Some narratives share small stories, such as an account of a single event.

One can also structure an essay around a *theme* or big idea, such as a characteristic you have. If you found a connection among your topic-testing quarterfinalists, that connection could bind your essay together. In Lia's essay (which you can read in the Appendix), her favorite hobbies seemed completely different and random to her until she realized they were all examples of her "inner biologist" at play. Her penchant for applying the scientific method to her life became her essay's theme.

I hope this oversimplification of two common essay structures helps you breathe easier. I really do. Though in practice, there are as many variations on essay structures as there are people. To complicate matters further, good essays include a narrative the reader can clearly follow *and* dip beneath the surface into a deeper theme.

For example, my student Levi, a classic pantser, wrote a

straightforward narrative about following fox footprints through snow on a winter's day in so much detail that reading it feels like a virtual reality experience. But his essay (which you can read in the Appendix, as well) also centered around themes in his life that drew him to activities he loved, like wildlife tracking, rock climbing, and computer science (his future college major).

Beginnings, Middles, and Endings

One-Third, One-Third, One-Third

While I cannot safely say all essays can be neatly categorized as either narrative or theme structured, I *can* safely say that every essay needs a beginning, middle, and ending. Let's keep it simple and think about planning your essay in thirds, like three snowballs piled on top of one another to look like a snowman (a snow plan!).

1. ***The first third is the beginning.*** Your goal is to grab your reader's attention.
2. ***The next third is the middle.*** Your goal is to keep your reader engaged.
3. ***The last third is the ending.*** Your goal is for your reader to exit your essay feeling like they know you better.

You can keep these proportions in mind, but don't be persnickety about trying to make each third perfectly even. *Ditch the idea of perfect altogether*, while you're at it. Some snow people have a smaller head, a thinner belly, or a middle that kind of melts into their base, an apt metaphor for the different ways this essay shape can go for you when you sit down to write. The differences are what make a snowman, a person, and an essay interesting.

I'm about to shower you with ideas for beginnings, middles, and endings, meant as *inspiration, not obligation* for your Parachute Plan. If one idea speaks to you, grab it, run with it, or mix and match with other ideas. Preparing a place to start, perhaps a place to end, and pantsing your way through the middle of your first draft is also a legitimate plan. You do you. When examples from successful essays written by real students show up in this chapter, please feel free to flip to the Appendix at any time to enjoy reading those completed essays with Parachute Planning in mind.

Beginnings

You can start *anywhere* when you're writing your first draft, since you'll shape it up when you revise. I offer you some fun, effective starting points to try.

Start where you feel like starting.

You always have the option of pantsing this essay right from the beginning, if that is your way. Start with the freewriting you did on your chosen topic in the Topic-Testing Quarterfinals and continue from there to discover where it leads.

Start with an anecdote.

Lots of successful essays begin with an *anecdote*, which is a fancy word for a little personal story. Your whole essay could be an anecdote (Tyler's entire essay takes place in three minutes), or an anecdote can serve as an example (see how each of Lia's middle paragraphs is a little story unto itself). If you enacted the Magical Shrinking Topic Trick until you reduced your essay topic to one moment, you may have ended up with an alluring anecdote to begin your essay.

Start with dialogue.

Begin with a couple of lines of dialogue, complete with quotation marks and *he saids*. No one expects you to remember the *exact* words, but starting with a conversation, as you remember it, delivers instant action. Emilio's opening provides a nice example of inserting dialogue. (Don't worry about perfect dialogue punctuation; we'll fix all that in chapter 12.)

Start with a vivid image.

Freeze a memory in your mind like a photograph, and re-create it with words, the way you'd stand on a riverbank with an easel re-creating a landscape with paint. Let your creative side loose and use the blank page as your canvas. If you venture beyond visuals to include your other senses, the scene will burst into three dimensions for your reader.

What if you begin with a question or hypothesis?

I'll bet you the reader will keep reading to learn the answer or outcome. That's how Evelyn's essay works at the beginning (and end).

Start with conflict.

Share a challenge, obstacle, or failure you faced…but don't wallow in the problem beyond the one-third mark. Spend at least two-thirds of your essay on the *aftermath*, how you dealt with difficulty, and what you learned from it. Melanie began her essay freaking out. But she devoted much more essay space overall to how she dealt with her anxiety than on describing the anxiety itself.

Break the rules.

Well, everyone knows you can't write about *urine* in your college essay (though that's exactly how Levi began his) or write in some made-up language (Priya) or in computer code (Billy) or include a math problem (Evelyn) or paint your essay into being (Cassidy).

Need I go on? Have a little fun and try writing in your *love language*, whether that's music or numbers or snippets of French.

Middles

Continue where it continues.

No pressure for pantsers to create some elaborate structure. You don't earn extra credit for making life difficult for yourself. It's usually easiest to start at the beginning, continue into the middle, and keep writing in chronological order until the end of your story. Your Parachute Plan's middle can include a couple of not-to-be missed highlights.

Think in scenes, not voice-over summaries (as if your essay were a movie).

In a full-length film, there may be time for a disembodied voice to explain everything that happened between scenes and to include a montage of the protagonist's whole life on the screen. You do not have time to summarize your life history or everything that happened between paragraphs in your short personal essay. Choose a few pivotal moments to touch on in your essay's middle. Then cut to the chase and plan to hop from scene to scene, as Lia and Cassidy did. Readers need less spoon-fed information than you might think. Later, if you find a transition between scenes necessary, you can always add it.

Look for connections.

When you think about the four topic ideas that most attracted you, does a *theme* in your life connect them? And when you *really* think about it, does that theme extend beyond these four ideas for you? Could that theme possibly apply to many (or all) of the activities and people you gravitate toward, as well as your plans for your future? (Is your mind blown yet?)

My student Sonia had an ADHD diagnosis and lived a hectic life in a big city. She contemplated the connection between two seemingly totally different activities she loved (and had tested in her quarterfinals), archery and gardening, and found that both were great examples of calm sanctuaries she sought to keep her mind and body grounded. What began as two separate essay topic ideas became illustrations of that one theme in Sonia's life. Your topic ideas that made the quarterfinals, and even some of your topic-testing freewriting, could now serve as great material for your middle paragraphs, as well.

Stay in the spotlight.

If you want to write about people, places, or causes that have influenced or inspired you, all good. Credit due to them, as long as you remain the star of your essay. Plan to include those inspirations in the middle of your essay, but don't let others steal the spotlight. This is *your* show!

Keep it personal.

Colleges are interested in how you landed on a prospective major or career ambition, so if relevant academics play a role in your college essay, that's appropriate. What colleges do *not* want is a pedantic tutorial on any subject, which is not the assignment. You may have encyclopedic knowledge of your topic. If so, please do contribute content to Wikipedia, but omit it from the middle of your personal essay. Instead, plan to share your *personal relationship* with the idea or concept so your essay doesn't sound like a research paper.

Find ideas in familiar places.

Hunt through all your chapter 4 exercises for discarded ideas you've already generated. As you read through your Mother Lode

Master List or your elimination rounds, you might happen upon one or more good ideas to incorporate into the middle of your essay.

Find ideas in new places.

Try a Brain Hurricane like you did in chapter 3 to conjure up new *specific*, personal moments related to your topic. These could become touchpoints to include in the middle of your Parachute Plan.

Be specific.

Specific = personal
General = generic

I'm sorry if you're sick of hearing this advice. I'll keep repeating it until my face turns purple because it's for your own good and for the good of your essay. Use the Magical Shrinking Topic Trick to make sure your middle ideas are as specific and personal as the topic they support.

Endings

Connect your ending to your beginning.

Think of your beginning and ending as a couple who have a strong relationship and make sense together. The beginning and ending are bookends holding together a row of books so one side doesn't topple over. The beginning is a call, while the ending is the response. You get the idea.

End where it ends.

If you're a pantser, you can keep writing through your first draft until the story ends with a punchline or fizzles out. Cleaning it up or finding a pithier conclusion is what revision is for.

End with an anecdote.

Does ending your story with another little story sound crazy? I say, why not try it? Or here's another wild idea: Plan to write part of an anecdote at the beginning, leave it hanging, and conclude the anecdote at the end to create essay *bookends*, as Lia did.

End on an image.

I don't know about you, but I love when I finish a good story and I'm left with a picture in my mind that sometimes lingers for the rest of the day. An image of you behaving like your genuine self may help the reader remember you better. Check out Tyler's ending as an example.

Answer the question.

If the starting question is *Why?*, reflect on the *reason* in your ending. If the starting question is *Who?* or *What?*, unveil the person, place, or thing at the end. If you begin with *Where?* or *When?*, you know what to do. Levi began with a question and ended his essay with why he cares about the answer.

Kneecap the recap.

In school, the five-paragraph essay famously ends with a full paragraph summary that mostly consists of what you already said. In a personal essay, there's a word for that: *repetitive*. You can reference your beginning and points you made along the way, but end your essay by helping the reader feel, see, or understand something *new* about you.

As an example, Priya's essay ended with a conversation reminiscent of the conversation at the beginning. However, by the end of her story, the dialogue takes on new meaning because we've learned how she grew from a hesitant first-year learning how to debate to a senior teaching the new first-year students how debate was done. (Plus, by the end of her essay we're in on the kooky language Priya used for debate success, so that's fun.)

End with the lesson.

Does your essay topic lead to a lesson learned? If so, share that lesson, but don't end your essay summarizing it. Try pushing it further. How have you *applied* that lesson to other parts of your life? How might you apply it to your future studies, career, or relationships? This is college-level inquiry and conjecture, and you are ready for it.

Reflect a layer deeper.

Apply your natural *curiosity* to your topic. You can go back to the Down the Reflection Rabbit Hole questions in chapter 3 and descend again into the warren to see if any of your previous answers change or stick. And you can add more questions to the mix.

- Why are you sharing all this in your personal essay?
- What makes this topic so fascinating to you?
- What will this essay reveal about you as a human?

Your answers to these big philosophical questions may be different from day to day (or moment to moment), or some questions may be ultimately unanswerable, but they're surely worth pondering when you're about to shift gears from high school to the next stage of your life.

Break the rules.

Experimentation is low-stakes here. Permission granted to have a little unconventional fun. Try ending with a question instead of an answer, a line of dialogue, another language that speaks to you (calculus? choreography? Cantonese?). Go earnest or meta. Crack a joke like Emilio did. If you become a little punchy and playful after you've been writing for a while, all the better. It's a sign that your inhibition has exited the room and creativity has entered.

Phew, that was a truckload of information and ideas. Let's take a sanity break before we pull it all together to concoct your plan.

Leaves on a Stream

Brain Booster: Estimated 3 Minutes

Consider this: Millions of thoughts enter your head every day. Your thoughts and fears and worries are not facts. They are not *you*. Instead of becoming entangled with your thoughts, you have the power to choose to believe them or not.

Instructions

1. Watch the ticker tape of thoughts flitting through your mind, without judgment.
2. Add *I'm thinking*...in front of each thought to gain some distance from it. For example, *I'm thinking I'm a little chilly. I'm thinking that I need a haircut. I'm thinking if I don't make a good Parachute Plan, I won't write a good essay or get into a good college or become a successful, happy person.* Hmmm. Interesting.
3. When your Inner Troll feeds you a thought you disagree with (like doomspiraling about what might happen if your Parachute Plan goes bust), visualize that unhelpful thought landing on a leaf floating down a gentle stream.
4. Watch it float away from you with the current,

receding, smaller and smaller until it disappears around a bend.

Bye-bye unhelpful thought. Your feelings are always valid, but your *thoughts* about those feelings are not necessarily reality. *Embrace your power* to place unconstructive thoughts on a leaf floating down a stream and out of your life forever. Namaste.

Sew Your Parachute Plan

Writing Exercise: Estimated 15 Minutes

Create a compass for your essay to keep you on track without holding back your adventurous spirit.

Instructions

- **Set a timer for 15 minutes** if you're a planner in danger of overthinking (you know if you are).
- **Use ideas for beginnings, middles, and endings** presented in this chapter for inspiration to fill in the blanks in the outline that follows.

Helpful Hints

- **Plan to reflect** on your topic, your theme, or both as part of your middle or ending. Leave yourself a little time and space for contemplation, but no need to stress over planning specifics. Reflecting more deeply starts as a spontaneous improvisation in the first draft for most students.
- **Keep perspective.** This plan is a safety measure for backup to refer to as needed while writing your *rough* essay draft. Sketch it out, then move along.

My topic: ____

____

____

Begin here: ____

____

____

Middle third(ish):

- Point 1: ____
- Point 2: ____
- Point 3: ____

End here: ____

____

____

You're prepared! You are the world's foremost expert on the unique topic of this essay, and now you have a plan.

Chapter 6

Blurt Your Essay into Being

First Draft FAQs

You have the power (you've had it all along).

In this chapter, you'll spew out a gloriously hot, tangled mess of words that's imperfect and probably way too long but captures your energy, spirit, and potential. A pep talk is in order.

Your job is to plant your butt in the chair and blurt out enough words to create an essay draft. No one is grading you on this. Getting this essay done well does not mean writing brilliantly. It means locking away your Inner Troll, letting any negative thoughts float away, and going for it. It means continuing to write from beginning to end, even when you feel a little stuck, even when you wander away from your Parachute Plan or make mistakes. It means saying what you want to say without worrying about what you think colleges want to hear.

Your first draft is just for you, not for your critics.

I'll answer the most frequently asked questions (FAQs) I hear from students about to embark on their first essay draft.

Why blurt out my first draft fast from start to finish?

I have my reasons for suggesting you try freewriting your first draft all the way through.

- This tactic leaves *no openings for your Inner Troll* to slither in and sabotage you.

- Your *authentic voice* will flow naturally when you're not concerned with perfectly arranging words on the page.
- The speed gives the writing *energy* that can't be matched when you write in a more calculated way.

If you have determined that speed freewriting is not for you, I respect that. Still, try to write your first draft all the way through in one sitting, and I recommend setting yourself a time limit to maintain efficiency.

How long should my draft be?

Shoot for longer than you'll need (if your first draft comes out as double the maximum word count, all good) because later, cutting can be easier than adding. However, don't sweat it if your first draft runs short. You'll have a chance to fatten it up with scrumptious details in draft 2.

What if I get stuck?

Fun fact: Most writers get stuck while they write, at least once.

You've collected tools in every chapter of this book so far to bolster you through those stuck spots.

- ***Keep writing through that stuck moment.*** Sentences that burst out next can yield the best, most magical surprises when you least expect them.
- ***Tune in to your five senses*** so you can record the endless specific details you're noticing.
- ***Use your Parachute Plan.*** When you hit a stuck place, all you need to do is pull the cord to transport you to the next planned point.
- ***Tap into your natural curiosity*** to reflect on why, out of all the topics you could've chosen, the universe led you to write about *this* today.

- ***Call upon Brain Booster tactics*** to regain perspective if your self-talk turns negative when you're stuck. Telling yourself *I am excited!* is an easy one to conjure in a pinch.

What if I veer away from my plan into the mysterious unknown?

Go with it! Another story longing to bubble to the surface might fizz out. Nothing you write today is unchangeable, so you have nothing to lose by trying something spontaneous.

I've never felt confident about my writing. How can I feel confident now?

Your thoughts, including assumptions about who you thought you were as a writer, are not facts. Observe your thoughts without adding judgments. *I'm thinking I'm a bad writer. Hmmm. That's interesting.* Place that thought on a leaf and watch your crisis of confidence float downstream, around the bend where you can no longer see it. This is a different type of writing than the usual writing you do for school, and you are as capable of excelling at it as anyone else.

But what if it doesn't feel good when I start writing, and the writing is forced, and bad, and my topic is horrible, and I'm too tired for this today, and I...?

Okay, we're doing this. Please stand in superhero position, feet hip width apart, hands on hips, chin up, and let what I'm about to tell you sink in.

- You were born prepared to share your story under *any* conditions.
- This is just a *first* draft, and it won't be your last.
- You are the expert on the topic of yourself, and the world is waiting to hear all about you.

I recommend you remain in your superhero power pose, cape fluttering behind you, for this next exercise.

The 333 Method to Topple Performance Anxiety

Brain Booster: Estimated 2 Minutes

Instructions

1. Look around at the world outside of your body and identify three objects.
2. Next identify three sounds.
3. Then move three body parts. (Extra points if you can wiggle your ears, JK.)

Have you climbed out of your head (and out of your own way) yet?

Now all you need to do is plant your butt in a chair, start typing, and see what happens. Have fun!

Write Like No One Will Ever See It (They Won't)

Writing Exercise: Estimated 45 Minutes
(but Set Aside an Hour)

You have your Parachute Plan (planner).
You have the freedom to depart from your plan if you damn well please (pantser).
No timer. No Inner Troll. Embrace your power.

Instructions

With your Parachute Plan as backup, you know where to begin. Write fast, blurting out an energetic, engaging (to you), authentic, *imperfect* hot mess of an essay draft in one sitting without stopping. Write like not a soul is watching (we aren't).

After you type your last word, *hands up, off the keyboard where I can see them.*

Don't touch that essay you just wrote. Don't even peek. This is for your essay's success as well as your mental health. Instead, own this huge (*huge*) accomplishment. You were intrepid. You were decisive. *You did the thing* and now you have an essay draft.

Celebrate Interim Wins

Brain Booster: Take 3 Minutes, 3 Hours, or the Time You Need to Feel This Success *in Your Bones*.

Do not let your accomplishments pass you by, no matter how big or small. Both business and mental health studies have shown that self-rewarding will propel you toward the next small victory, and the next, to achieve big wins.

Instructions

Pick from the reward list below or choose your own way to celebrate *right now*.

Reward Ideas

- Ice cream (of course).
- Bake cookies (and win friends by sharing them). Everybody celebrates!
- Savor a cup of hot tea (add honey).
- Take a walk or run (bonus points if you don't plug in).
- Enter all-out pamper mode with face mask, pedicure, bubble bath, the works.

- Crank up your favorite song, and dance (or listen with no other distractions).
- Do your own thing as a reward, but make sure it's an out-of-the-ordinary treat.

Ease the Transition to Revision

Tip 1: Sleep on your first draft (again, well done).

Don't peek at what you wrote for as long as you can stand it. That way, when you return to your draft, you can see it more clearly than at this moment when your heart still races with the adrenaline rush of creation.

If you've already read through your draft, no shame. Please put it aside before you change anything. With a little distance, you'll return to what you've written with much clearer vision. This tip alone will save you *so much time* and headaches later.

Tip 2: Save draft 1 (and later, draft 2 and draft 3) in all its imperfect glory before you change a word.

Leave draft 1 intact and make a copy to use for your revisions. Save a copy of each new draft before you move on to the next. I've known too many students over the years who wished they could have gone back to a thought or sentence they'd captured in an earlier draft that was gone forever. It's a lot easier to make necessary, sometimes ruthless cuts when you know those words still exist somewhere in case you happen to need them again.

Tip 3: Maintain a glass-half-full attitude to save time and energy.

Don't let your Inner Troll be a hater of any part of your first draft. No one on this green earth births a perfect essay on their first try. You have three more drafts to address all those things you're wondering (or worried) about and make changes. Continue your forward momentum instead of second-guessing what you've already achieved.

Tip 4: Invest in your future by scheduling time for revision.

I know for sure from years of experience that students who submit a first draft (or a first draft with cursory corrections) as part of their college application fool no one. Evaluators question those students' work ethic — not a good look. If you've never spent much time revising school papers and don't know where to begin, I've got you covered. I'll guide you step-by-step in the chapters ahead with efficient exercises, so you'll stay on course and also have a life. (You're welcome.) But it's up to you to carve out time for revision on your calendar. You are worth the investment.

Tip 5: Hold off on sharing your draft.

You might face external pressure from people in your life who genuinely want to help. But your messy, energetic, inspired, authentic, partially formed essay draft is in no shape to share with anyone yet. A critique of a rough draft you haven't yet had the chance to revise can unleash your Inner Troll with a vengeance. If you find one of your allies on your college admissions journey hungrily circling, hoping to glimpse your essay-in-progress, and you aren't sure how to stave them off, assistance is here.

Dragon Training (aka Fending Off the Persistently Curious)

I told you no one would ever see your first draft for two reasons.

1. I hoped to lower the stakes so you could just write the thing (and you did).

2. No one *should* see your first draft. You haven't even had the chance to truly see it yourself yet.

Still, persistently curious people might pester you to show them that document you just wrote. Let's not call it your *essay* yet because it is far from fully formed. They'll tell you they only want to read it, that they won't say a word, and they will mean it. Yet despite their best intentions, if they see what you've written, they will reveal their opinion — whether it's with a tight-lipped half smile you know well or words they cannot hold inside. Aunts, cousins, grandparents, neighbors, friends, or that competitive guy you hardly know in your AP US History class might be curious and impressively persistent, but I mostly field complaints from students about pressure coming from their parents.

When the Persistently Curious Person Is a Parent

If a parent is asking (or pushing) to read your essay draft, they will believe their bursting-at-the-seams interest is about your college essay. However, it's really about the depth of their love for you. I hope I can convince you to feel empathy for your devoted parents. When you were born, they swore to protect you, and they are desperate to continue protecting you now. They believe in their hearts that it's up to them to make sure the world sees the amazing human they know you are. They believe they are fulfilling their parenting oath by making sure your essay captures you the way they see their beloved child.

They also want to feel needed because very soon, you'll leave the secure nest they've built for you to forge your own path in the world. Your poor parents' primary job has slowly evolved from protecting you at all costs to teaching you to protect yourself to letting you go make your own way in the world. Let me tell you as a parent myself, when it finally strikes us that our role has shifted from protector to supporter (sometimes after we drop you off at college), it feels like headbutting against the brutal recognition that one stage of *our* life has ended and another has begun, a similar rite of passage to the one that is happening for you.

It's not you who needs your parents to reassure you about your essay. It's your parents who need you to reassure them about their parenting.

How You Can Help Your Suffering Parents

Your parents are used to setting boundaries with you, but they are not used to you setting boundaries for them. This is simply a fact of parenting, *not a bad thing about your parents*. If a parent is hounding you about your essay, you must set some boundaries, as they've done for you all these years. When you do, please be gentle and kind (they are fragile).

Setting boundaries requires resolve and clarity, yet it's helpful to sprinkle some sugar as you ease into your request. Acknowledge that the persistently curious parent has done a wonderful job raising you (of course, they have), and because of their outstanding parenting, you're a capable, independent person who can do this on your own. Request they please let you try. Explain to them that your writing is not ready for human consumption yet. This doesn't mean you will never show anyone your essay. What it means is that it's your choice when you're ready.

I've heard from students about parents who go to great lengths to convince their child they know them best (actually, you know yourself best), that their child needs parental input to make sure the essay is good (it is *not* good yet, you can inform them if it comes to this, but reassure them it will be great eventually). What those parents are really doing is trying to convince their kid and themselves that their child still needs them, period. (You can tell them you will always need them, only differently than you did when you were younger.)

There Will Come a Time for Sharing

Now is not the time to relent to the persistently curious and share your newborn essay. Your Inner Troll is the sole being who will benefit if you share your rough first essay draft. However, I will encourage you in chapter 13 to share your essay. By then you'll have much more knowledge about what you need from your readers and Reader's Guidelines to make sure you'll receive *productive* rather than destructive feedback.

If You're on Your Own

If you are winding your way through copious college admissions advice, standardized testing, researching colleges, pulling together pieces of your college application, and writing your essay with no guidance at all from parents or anyone else, you are a superstar, and I am your biggest fan. I am also thrilled you picked up this book so I can be here for you as you flip through the pages.

Please understand, if you're not receiving support from the adults in your life, that does not mean they don't want to support you. It could mean either they don't know how to help or they *are* silently supporting you by remaining hands-off because they trust your competency. Another possibility is you haven't asked. You have people waiting in the wings — whether a parent, another relative, teachers, counselors, friends, or an adviser outside of school like a coach or clergy member — to help when you need it *if you ask*. This is a friendly reminder we can't read minds.

I hope you feel proud of all you've accomplished so far. Coming right up, some shiny new tools for your adventure in revision…

Part III

DRAFT 2 — THE BIG PICTURE

Chapter 7

RE-ENVISION

Conquer the Point of Most Resistance

Hey Ms. Shulman,

Sorry to bother you, but I just read over my first draft, and I feel like I'm doing all of this wrong. I think I should try a different topic. Could you suggest a couple more from my list that also seem promising for me to write about? I'm not very good at themes or messages, but I'm worried that this topic might not lead to an essay that shows anything about me. I feel like maybe the story that would make a great essay just isn't actually there in this topic. Or, maybe it is, but in that case, I feel like I'm having trouble finding the details/interpreting the situation correctly in order to bring it out. Maybe this is normal, but I don't want to get too far into revising an essay with a topic I'm not feeling.

Thanks,

Lia

Oh Lia,

You can't do this wrong. There is no "interpreting the situation correctly" or themes or messages to worry about right now. Remember, this is creative writing, not a research paper. You are way overthinking it.

You don't have to choose the perfect topic. It usually starts with some random detail that popped into your freewriting and surprised you, not some big, dramatic moment. Go figure. The point of writing super-fast without stopping is so you don't give yourself a chance to hesitate and let this kind of self-doubt seep in.

And yes, this is so normal. It's called your *Inner Troll!* Go back to the playful headspace you were in when you freewrote your way into an intriguing topic and your brilliant hot mess of a first draft (it really is fantastic). Right now, we need your Inner Superhero to drown out the intrusions of he-who-shall-not-be-named and revisit what you've already written with realism, not black-and-white thinking. Some parts of your first draft will have great potential, and others not so much. Remember how the right frame of mind was everything for writing a kick-ass personal essay draft? The same goes for revising.

You must be firm. Escort your Inner Troll back to its jail cell and add an extra padlock to the door. It's for his trollship's own good, and yours. Doubt has been excommunicated from the room. You have made space for an objective, optimistic read-through of your first draft and for your Inner Superhero's voice to ring across the land, "You have everything it takes. Let's do this!"

All my best,

Jill

To: Jill

Thank you!

Lia

You have already conquered getting started, the biggest challenge most students face. Now comes the next big hurdle. For many students, like Lia, switching gears from creating the first essay draft to revising the second is the point of *most* resistance in the whole essay writing process. Lia vaulted this hurdle; she just needed a little confidence boost. In the Appendix, you can find Lia's completed essay, which, despite her initial fears, shares oodles about her.

No matter how you feel about your first draft, you will leap this hurdle too. In this chapter, we'll begin by looking at the *big picture*. What have you already written? What is working? You must make the conscious choice to approach your first draft searching for its *successes* because your Inner Troll can find countless gaping flaws, as Lia's did.

Common Inner Troll trash talk sounds like *My essay is bad*, *I chose the wrong topic*, or, conversely, *If I touch what I wrote, I'll ruin it.* I call BS. Look, your first draft may be far too long, it may be all over the place, and you may not even be sure what it's about. But *future you* will thank *present you* for giving your first draft a chance by completing an honest self-assessment exercise later in this chapter.

By the way, you'll notice I've eliminated estimated time for the exercises from here on out. If you thrive on setting a timer, I trust you'll continue to do so.

Gratitude Journal

Writing Exercise

Let's start your revision journey with a moment of gratitude for *past you*, who already wrote the first draft of your college essay. Studies show that spending a few minutes focused on gratitude, especially when expressing it in writing, produces a chemical shift in your brain away from anxiety and toward good vibes.

Instructions

Write down five things you're grateful for, big or small. I'll start you out.

1. Essay draft accomplished!
2. ______________________
3. ______________________
4. ______________________
5. ______________________

Optional but good for your heart: Write for a couple more minutes about why you're grateful for one item on your gratitude list. If it involves a living creature (a friend, a parent, a teacher, a puppy), you can share what you've written with them and make their day. Set aside a few minutes to repeat this gratitude journal exercise tomorrow (and every day) if you like how it feels.

Five Common Revision Myths Busted

If you have reached junior or senior year in high school without fully understanding expectations regarding revision, I've got you now. False preconceived notions abound. It's time to set the record straight so we can move along to an effective revision process you can use for all your writing *forever*.

Myth 1: Revision means correcting spelling and punctuation.

Well, mechanical corrections are part of revision, but proofreading for mistakes doesn't come until the end of your writing escapades. If you're tempted to fix a few typos and commas on your first draft and call it a day, instead say, *Shut up, Inner Troll. I'm busy.* Proceed to give all steps of the revision process the respect and attention they merit.

Myth 2: Revision means a total rewrite.

This is Lia-style, extreme planner, black-and-white thinking. In this chapter we'll look for what's working with a combination of optimism and realism. In the chapters that follow, you'll decide which parts need rewriting. Some will, but not all.

As you know, I recommend forward momentum, but this is *your* essay, not mine. I will not shame you if it will give you peace of mind to take a step backward and start with a different quarterfinalist topic or start again from scratch. Your time is currency to spend as you wish, so I say what I'm about to say with so much love in my heart. *Spending extra time moving backward instead of forward is not evidence of a stellar work ethic* (as your Inner Troll might tempt you to believe). Second-guessing is more likely a symptom of fear than a symptom of a failed essay draft. Knowing this, if you have the time to spare to start over, go wild and enjoy! But please, before you do, objectively assess your first draft in the next writing exercise, How Is Your Essay (So Far)?

Myth 3: My Inner Troll can actually help me when it comes to revision.

That's a hard no. You never, *ever* need your Inner Troll's downer attitude. This is the point in your writing adventure when your Inner Editor steps in, a whole different animal with a *positive* slant toward all you can do to make your essay drafts sparkly. (Do you remember meeting your Inner Editor in the Introduction?)

Myth 4: Someone else needs to read my first draft to make sure I'm on the right track before I spend time on revisions.

As with choosing a topic, your own excitement is a better indicator of whether this is a good working draft than Aunt Lucy's opinion (or her alternative idea she thinks colleges will like). When you've gone as far as you can with revisions on your own, it will be appropriate and important to share your essay along with the guidelines I'll provide to guarantee that your reader feedback will be beneficial and not debilitating.

Myth 5: The fun, creative, right-brain part of the writing process is done. Revision is a left-brain chore.

Heavens, no! You've been using both sides of your brain all along in parts I and II of this book. Your free-flowing, creative right brain helped you awaken your Inner Essayist and conjure up ideas. Your more practical left brain helped you keep records of your discoveries and make decisions. You'll continue to use your full brainpower, including the fun side (which could go either way, right or left), in part III and beyond. I pinkie swear I will not skimp on fun when it comes to making revision easy for you.

How Is My Essay (So Far)?

Writing Exercise

Please keep in mind, writing your first draft was a victory, no matter what. Use the following true-or-false self-assessment quiz to appraise what's working in the writing you have already done and what you'll want to focus on in the chapters ahead.

1. I care about the topic and enjoyed writing my first draft.

- ❑ **True:** Enthusiasm is contagious! If you were engaged in writing about a topic you genuinely care about, there's a strong chance the reader will care about it too.

- ❑ **False:** We can investigate why not in the pages that follow. Maybe a different approach to the same topic would excite you more. You'll have opportunities to explore that option.

2. I had lots to say on this topic, and it was easy to come up with details to share.
- ❑ **True:** If your answer was a resounding yes, outstanding!
- ❑ **False:** If not, please don't give up on your essay yet. Your topic may be fine, but if you ran out of ideas while writing, it may still be too broad. The solution could be as simple as narrowing down your topic more as you revise. The Magical Shrinking Topic Trick from chapter 4 will continue to come in handy.

3. This essay reveals more about me as a person, beyond my activities, grades, and accomplishments.
- ❑ **True:** If you wrote from your heart, the reader will see that you are much more than your achievements and the activities you've done. We all are.
- ❑ **False:** When you think about it, if the content of draft 1 mostly repeats your activities or achievements that readers will learn about in other parts of your application, please don't worry. In draft 2 you can rework parts to include new, personal information.

4. My future college major or clubs I want to join would make sense to the reader after they read this essay.
- ❑ **True:** Most college admission evaluators will read your whole application all at once. If your essay draft would fit into the "holistic" picture of you already forming in readers' minds but also enhance it, great!
- ❑ **False:** If your essay doesn't add to your application's big picture yet, during revisions we'll work on making sure you capture the real you in all your multifaceted glory.

5. Other people might appear in this essay, but the spotlight is on me.
- ❑ **True:** Terrific. Just double-checking.
- ❑ **False:** Some students find it easier to write about an influential person, community, or cause than about themselves. Does that describe you? If so, a good, easy place to start revisions is to make sure the capital letter *I* appears all over the place in draft 2.

6. Someone who knows me could easily recognize that I wrote this essay.
- ❑ **True:** If your genuine voice came out to play in draft 1, I love that for you.
- ❑ **False:** If the voice sounds more formal than you usually do (like the one you would use for persuasive school papers or job interviews), in draft 2 you can start to replace stiffer language with words you'd actually use in conversation.

7. I was curious about exploring this topic on a deeper level, and I still am.
- ❑ **True:** A good essay is engaging. A *great* essay takes a deep dive beneath the surface story into reflection about the topic. If you attempted some deeper reflection, even if it came out as gibberish, that is enough for draft 1.
- ❑ **False:** Remember that your first draft is only the beginning of the pondering you'll do as you travel through your revisions. You know when you read or hear something you've always taken for granted (or found boring), but looking at it from a new perspective suddenly makes it fascinating? Consider what you've written from different angles. Viewing it through a new lens might spark your curiosity in passages that looked mundane at first glance.

8. This essay shows how I've grown, learned, or changed.
- ❑ **True:** Well done if you've already put some thought

into how you've changed and matured as it relates to your topic. Your ability to learn from your past experiences and apply those lessons to your present life shows evaluators you will make the most of your college experience in the future.

❏ **False:** If you spent more of your essay space explaining a challenge or obstacle you faced than how you grew from it, the bones of your essay might already exist, but the proportions might be off. Remember the snowman shape of one-third, one-third, one-third from chapter 5? Upcoming exercises will help you tweak those proportions.

9. If I were a stranger meeting me for the first time through reading this essay, I think I'd like me.

❏ **True:** If the voice in this essay represents the way you really are, I'm sure any reader would like you (and want to fight for you in an admissions committee).

❏ **False:** If you tried to write what you thought would impress colleges, it may come across in a tone that's not yours. If you recognize a discrepancy, it can still work out because tone is fixable, as you'll see in chapter 10.

10. I was open and honest when I wrote my first draft, even when it meant showing vulnerability.

❏ **True:** I'm glad you understand that no one is perfect, including admission evaluators, who will relate to you best (and recommend you for admission) when you're genuine, warts and all.

❏ **False:** In case you momentarily forgot, no one will ever see draft 1, and the same goes for draft 2. You're in a judgment-free zone between the covers of this book, where you can practice opening up and expressing your authentic self or delete any oversharing that makes you cringe as you wind through revision exercises.

Tally: True ______ False ______

A Moment of Reckoning Before You Proceed

Just being real here: If you answered more of the statements in the How Is Your Essay (So Far)? quiz with "false" than "true," and you're unhappy with your first draft, there's no one-size-fits-all way to proceed.

I want you to feel validated to say what you want to say. Take an extra beat to accept the human condition of imperfection before you discard your first draft. If you still feel dissatisfied, have the time and wherewithal, and think attempting a new first draft might boost your enthusiasm and faith in yourself, I'm supportive.

If you're inclined to take a step backward before moving forward, I'd hate to see you waste one second of your precious time, so here are a couple of *efficiency shortcuts*.

- ***Option 1:*** Take three minutes to go back to chapter 1 and revisit the Inner Troll Exorcism exercise to make sure trying a different direction is really what you want and isn't your Inner Troll at work. Just sayin'.
- ***Option 2:*** Circle back to the Topic-Testing Quarterfinals in chapter 4. Then move forward trying a different topic you've already generated and vetted. The beauty of this book is that all upcoming exercises will still be here waiting for you whenever you return.

Practice Imperfection

Brain Booster

Maintain your sense of humor and humility and have fun doing something totally new for you. What's the worst that could happen? I can answer with confidence that nothing terrible will result, which is why practicing imperfection will make you stronger and braver.

- If you are in no way an artist, try sketching an animal, vegetable, or mineral you can see right now.
- If you are not an athlete, try jogging two hundred yards.
- If you're not a singer, sing the chorus of your favorite song out loud (even if you can't carry a tune).
- If you're a squirmy person, sit still and meditate for one whole minute.
- If you can't cook, fry an egg.
- If you've never thought you could __________ [fill in the blank], try it.

Notice that you strayed far, far away from your comfort zone and you're still here to laugh about it. Now lower your expectations about what you might find in your first draft because you're about to plunge into your first read-through.

Hunt for Treasure

Writing Exercise

Glittering gems will reveal themselves when you begin mining. Read through your first draft looking for what's working. A college admission evaluator will search for reasons to like what you've written, and so should you.

Instructions

As you read through your essay for the first time, *highlight your essay's successes* in your favorite color. (I gravitate toward emerald green.)

Helpful Hints

- **Focus on what is working,** no matter how small.
- **Highlight parts that come alive for you** and hold your attention. *Fun fact:* Whatever attracts your attention will attract your reader's attention too.
- **Highlight passages that make you feel something inside** — anything funny, moving, insightful, or thoughtful is worth noting.
- **Be generous with yourself** and your highlights. Highlight paragraphs, sentences, even single words that seem remotely promising and could prove useful in the coming drafts.
- **No judging yourself on the quantity of highlights.** If you find yourself highlighting almost every word, or not much at all, this draft is still a win because you leaped the massive hurdle of getting started. Congratulate yourself. You're on your way.

Treasure unearthed! Rev your forklift and your courage because we're off to the construction zone…

Chapter 8

Enter the Construction Zone — Move and Remove

Build a Frankenstein's Monster Draft

"My ADHD makes my writing disorganized," Sonia said of her first-draft freewriting, which pulsed with energy, enthusiasm, fresh ideas, and stunning sentences she'd plopped onto the page in no particular order.

It took a little convincing for Sonia to believe this word salad of a first draft was *okay*. When you read Sonia's fully developed essay in the Appendix, you'd never know draft 1 flopped around on the page like a wild puppy in need of training. No matter what your first draft looks like right now — more lowlights than highlights, mistakes radiating from sentences, no structure to speak of — we'll start making sense of all those words and begin arranging them in this chapter.

In Mary Shelley's classic novel *Frankenstein*, the mad scientist Dr. Frankenstein gathered body parts from corpses and animals and screwed them together to create a hideous creature. Dr. Frankenstein's monster did not start out mean. The creature soured when he attempted to make friends but was misunderstood. If only humans had given that creature the benefit of the doubt, *as you will do with your essay*, his fate (not good) might have turned out differently.

Fun fact: Your essay will grow uglier before it becomes the beauty you're proud to show anyone, let alone colleges.

Your second draft is destined to develop into a bit of a monster as you move, remove, add, and substitute large chunks of words from draft 1 and begin to screw the pieces together. The goal for this chapter is to cobble together essay parts into a form with a head at the top, feet at the bottom, and a torso and limbs placed somewhere in between. We're looking at the big picture — your essay as a whole. This is no time for nitpicking. Please don't let your Inner Troll cast aspersions on the draft 2 creature you create.

As a reminder, *becoming more comfortable with the uncomfortable is part of the adventure.*

Order Your Essay Around

Abandon the Plan

I'm sure you had lovely aspirations in your Parachute Plan. I hope that plan helped you feel protected as you wrote your first draft. You can let go of it now. Look at what you *have*, not what you planned to have, as you rearrange hunks of your essay.

Essay Structure Recap

- Every essay needs a *beginning* to wake up the college application reader who may already have read thirty-five essays that day, a *middle* that keeps the reader awake, and an *ending* that leaves your reader understanding something new about you.
- Proportionally, think roughly one-third beginning, one-third middle, and one-third ending.
- A straightforward *narrative* means you start at the beginning and unfurl your story in chronological order until you reach its natural conclusion.
- Organizing around a *theme* means that a central idea,

concept, or special characteristic you have threads your essay together. Paragraphs include personal experiences and anecdotes to support that big idea.

- I'm hopeful you'll end up with a clear narrative that includes a beginning, middle, and ending, *as well as* a deeper theme in your essay.

Ideas for What You Can Move to the Beginning

- ***Start in the clear.*** Nothing loses a reader's attention more quickly than confusion. Sometimes clear trumps snappy. Levi's essay in the Appendix begins with "Snow tracking is hard." Not fancy, but it does the trick. Did you write a no-frills, clear sentence you can move up to the top of your essay?
- ***Start where your highlights begin.*** Snagging your reader's interest is a goal at the beginning of your essay, so look at the spot where *you* snapped to attention. That might be a great place to begin.
- ***Start with the best anecdote.*** Maybe you began with an anecdote but wrote a better one after you warmed up. Why not move the most captivating anecdote to the beginning to start your essay with a bang?
- ***Begin with half the story.*** Did you start with an anecdote or a conversation? Try leaving only part of the story at the beginning. Does it make you want to read on to learn what happened? If so, move the rest of the story down for a satisfying ending (this method worked for Lia's essay). But if leaving only half of the story at the beginning seems confusing instead of enticing, paste the whole anecdote back together again. Don't be shy about experimenting.
- ***Rearrange backstory and scene.*** If you started draft 1 with lots of context or background information before

the action began, try swapping the order. Move the cluster of words where action started (perhaps where your highlights began) to the top of the page. Plopping us into the middle of a scene-in-progress is an exciting way to begin.

- ***Speak your love language.*** Priya's essay began with a secret debate language. Billy's essay began with a line of code. To kick off your essay, try a line written in Latin or scientific notation or whatever language speaks loudest to you.

Ideas for Moving Around the Middle

- ***When in doubt, arrange chronologically.*** Chronological order is usually the easiest, clearest way to organize, whether you're structuring a whole essay or the middle portion. You'll win no extra points for making your essay's structure complicated.
- ***Step back in time after the beginning.*** As an example, look at the way Priya's essay in the Appendix began with a scene in the present, then jumped back in time to share all the backstory that led to that moment.
- ***House the orphans.*** If some sentences or paragraphs you highlighted don't have a home yet, try slipping them into the middle in the order they happened. (Or move them to the bottom of the document, perhaps in position for the chopping block.)
- ***Get creative with braids and weaves.*** If a theme ties your essay together, your middle paragraphs will provide examples of that theme in action. Try interlacing a couple of those examples, like Melanie, Lia, and Sonia did in their essays. Reflection on the connections between seemingly very different pieces of your life can often work like a scrunchie linking them together at the end.

- ***Patch together freewriting to build your own creature.*** Did you find a theme connecting some of your favorite freewritings? Try plunking paragraphs you already freewrote (in your Topic-Testing Quarterfinals or a different writing exercise) into the middle of your essay to support the overarching theme that's developing. No worries about beauty, smoothing out transitions, or adding details now (that's what chapter 9 is all about).

Ideas for What Could Appear at the End

- ***Give a nod to the beginning.*** In chapter 5, I mentioned that your beginning is like a *call* and your ending a *response* — they're related. If you began with a problem, try moving the solution to the end. If you started with an anecdote, finish it or refer to it at the end.
- ***Don't stay a stranger.*** At the beginning of your essay, the reader doesn't know you yet. By the end, your goal is for the reader to better understand something fundamental to you. If during your Hunt for Treasure you highlighted words that expressed well what you were trying to say about who you are at your core, moving them to the end could drill in your point.
- ***End with a punch.*** Some of the best prose comes right after a point when you're stuck, but you continue writing anyway. Maybe you were a little tired or punchy, let your guard down, joked around, or added a comment in parentheses as an aside to yourself as you wrote. Try planting a line you wrote spontaneously at the end of your essay. Those unguarded moments can yield greater insight into your personality and perhaps leave the reader with a glimpse of who you really are.
- ***End in contemplation.*** In the thick of writing your draft,

did you articulate (or surprise yourself with) a cool idea? Did you have a profound moment of self-discovery? (It happens.) Upon reflection, did you stumble upon a theme that ties ideas together? Try moving that surprising, philosophical, or thoughtful paragraph or sentence to the end.

A Case Study in Rearranging the Beginning of an Essay

After Sonia highlighted the parts of her first draft that buzzed for her in the Hunt for Treasure exercise, her beginning looked like this:

> Every detail of the kyudo routine is planned out, down to which foot I step with first when retrieving an arrow from the target. These steps are all conducted with intention. In any form of archery, a consistent and specific routine is important to have a consistent shot direction, whether that be on target or off. When this consistent direction is achieved, all you have to do to hit your target is to change your aim.
>
> As much as a kyudo routine involved the basics of knocking your arrow or drawing the bow, there is an ever-present emphasis on the importance of how physical movements, groundedness, and relaxation, go along with mental stability and calm that shift my usually fast-paced, student-in-the-city thoughts. The routine leads with an open stance. I anchor myself in place, my lower body firm and aligned, feet rooting into the ground like a tree. My spine and head stretch to the sky like being pulled with a thread. I unclench my jaw and shoulders but stay activated with round ballerina arms that could hold an invisible ball of energy. My mind mimics this

> physical routine, becoming grounded and balanced with slow, natural breaths.

Sonia moved sentences around, so most of her highlights from her Hunt for Treasure read-through appeared in her first paragraph like this:

> I anchor myself in place, my lower body firm and aligned, feet rooting into the ground like a tree. My spine and head stretch to the sky like being pulled with a thread. I unclench my jaw and shoulders but stay activated with round ballerina arms that could hold an invisible ball of energy. My mind mimics this physical routine, becoming grounded and balanced with slow, natural breaths that shift my usually fast-paced, student-in-the-city thoughts.

She moved the remaining highlighted phrase all you have to do to hit your target is to change your aim down to use as part of a knockout ending.

All the unhighlighted sentences from Sonia's original beginning dangled in waiting for a home or for the chopping block. (You can see from her completed essay in the Appendix that most of those unhighlighted words ended up chopped.)

Box Breathing

Brain Booster

Before you begin your essay reconstruction project, this breathing technique can lower your blood pressure, reduce stress, improve concentration, and restore emotional balance, or at least the National Institutes of Health thinks so.

Instructions

1. Take a giant full-belly breath, counting to four as you inhale.
2. Hold that breath for four counts.
3. Exhale for four counts.
4. Hold on empty for four counts.

Repeat as needed until you feel grounded and ready because it's time to bust a move.

Reminder: Make sure you've saved a copy of your original draft 1 before making changes in the next exercise.

Head, Shoulders, Knees, and Toes (Move)

Writing Exercise

Instructions

Move words you wrote in draft 1 to better locations.

Helpful Hint

If your essay is already in a good order, no law says you need to fix something that isn't broken. You have the option to leave well enough alone, unsheathe your machete, and advance to *removal* (aka the bloodbath) up next.

War Strategy for Removal

"I'm not sure what to keep or what to cut," Sonia told me after her first read-through. If you're wondering the same thing, I'm here for you.

Fun fact: The biggest mistake students make when it's time to start cutting down their draft is to remove all the good stuff.

The most engaging parts that make an essay *personal* are the closely observed details that lead readers to feel like they're part of the story. When too many details are cut and only practical information remains, all that's left is a lifeless summary of facts. That method may prove effective when writing an abstract for your scientific research, but it's a death knell for a personal essay's impactfulness.

Advice for What You Can Cut

- ***Cut lots of the leftover words you didn't highlight.*** Let's face it; those words were already dead. You may be left with a mere skeleton of a draft, but you can add new flesh to it in chapter 9.
- ***Cut most of the voice-over summaries (and leave the scenes).*** If this essay is the movie of your life, make it action-packed. Were you fully immersed in the scene — mind, body, and soul — taking the reader by the hand and describing intricate details so the reader can join your world for a moment? If so, keep it. Then after your lovely scene, did you provide a synopsis of what you wanted the reader to learn from it? If so, cut the explication part.
- ***Cut words that veer off topic.*** Hold your breath and press *delete.*
- ***Cut phrases or even paragraphs that repeat.*** Do two sentences in a row say basically the same thing using different words? Cut one of them.
- ***Cut warm-up words from the beginning that you don't need anymore.*** If your highlights begin a few sentences or halfway into your first draft, that sea of words before the

highlights may have served as a warm-up for you. Lots of students *write into* their beginning, as Sonia found she had. As a bonus, in the future you'll know you might need to write for a few minutes as a little warm-up to help you reach the good stuff in all your writing. Self-knowledge is power. Cut those warm-up sentences if you haven't already moved them.

- ***Slice off extra words at the end of your essay.*** If your ending fizzles, try ending your essay earlier for a punchier finale. (If you can't bear to amputate those extra words, you can always move them elsewhere for now.)
- ***Trim the one-third that's out of proportion.*** If your opening anecdote or a middle example goes on too long, you know what to do. (In chapter 9, you can *add* to the parts of your essay you shortchanged in the first draft.)
- ***Cut to the chase.*** Readers are smart and need less backstory and context than many think. Give your readers the benefit of the doubt and cut most of the explaining that will bore them, or worse, come across as condescending.
- ***Cut definitions down to the minimum.*** Whittle any definitions of words or concepts down to the bare essentials.
- ***Sever preconceived ideas that didn't fly.*** If you followed your Parachute Plan but part of what you wrote didn't work out and feels stilted, cut that part now. Hooray for trying! Now buh-bye.
- ***Trim fat wherever you see it.*** Don't worry about word count. After the bloodbath, your essay may remain swollen or become much skinnier than 650 words. Be bold. Be ruthless. Your essay will sprout again with new growth in chapter 9.

Expired Words Graveyard (Remove)

Writing Exercise

Instructions

Lift your blade and slice out all the words no longer serving a purpose in your essay.

A Silent Meditation (with Gratitude for Draft 1 Words That Have Completed Their Service)

Brain Booster

Please join me for a moment of silence to honor the deserving words that supported your essay's creation. Not all of them lived to see the end of this chapter. They perished as heroes fighting for the cause of your knockout college essay. Amen.

Moving and removal complete. Does your essay look pretty? Not yet. Should you suppress your Inner Troll, trust the process, and push forward to *adding* and *substituting* up next? You betcha!

Chapter 9

Enhance — Add and Substitute

Time Travel Tutorial

"My English teacher told me to 'show, don't tell.' Did I do that?" my student Max asked me about the excerpt below from the first draft of his essay.

> I suddenly found myself living in a large, fancy, yellow, Colonial house in a more-or-less typical American suburb. Hanover, Massachusetts is a small, somewhat rural town twenty or so miles south of Boston. In many ways I think I lived a typical American kid lifestyle.

Why Adding a String of Adjectives Does Not Count as Showing

I could see why Max thought he was *showing*. Didn't "large, fancy, yellow, Colonial" show his house? Didn't "Hanover, Massachusetts" and "somewhat rural" make it specific?

I had to break it to Max that these details did not help me learn anything *personal* about him. Anyone who has ever moved to any suburb from anywhere that's *not* a suburb could have written those three sentences with word substitutions here and there. The house could've been a small, modest, blue Cape in Punxsutawney, Pennsylvania. *More-or-less typical* was the operative phrase in Max's sentences.

Max took this news like a champ. "So if that's not showing, what is?" he asked.

Max had no idea where to begin *adding* and *substituting* to show himself better in draft 2. If you're feeling the same way, strap on your space suit because time travel is the answer.

How to Break the Space-Time Continuum

Way back in chapter 2 you shelved your phone and replaced its blue light with *life.* Your Inner Essayist bolted upright to attention. Do you remember what it felt like to awaken your Inner Essayist? When you fully immersed yourself in the present moment, using all your senses, the IRL world (as it had existed all along) appeared to you. There was so much to notice! All you had to do was record what you saw (heard, smelled, tasted, touched, and were thinking) to create a virtual reality–like experience for anyone reading. Do you remember all that? You can apply those same powers of intense observation you unlocked in chapter 2 to notice what you're noticing about moments you experienced in the past.

Max, a practical guy by nature, gamely zipped into his zero-gravity suit and lowered his space helmet over his head. Pull up a chair and let Max beam you back to the moment he awoke for the first time in his new room in Hanover, Massachusetts.

> I had never been in such a big, colorful house before, with so many hallways and rooms that it felt like a maze. I was used to living in a building with uniform eggshell-white walls and beds lined up in rows of five. It felt strange sleeping alone; I couldn't look to my right and see my best friend, Ruseron. Instead, I looked to my right to find my very own white alarm clock sitting on my wooden nightstand in my new personal room.

Max's added details revealed that he wasn't just some kid who moved out of the city. He moved to the American suburbs when he was adopted from a Russian orphanage at age four. Now that he included the *real* specifics, it became a story only Max could write.

Why a Self-Conscious Description — as If You Were Someone Else Watching You — Is Not Authentic Showing

In his first draft, Max had described his suburban house from the *outside*, with a chain of adjectives — *large*, *fancy*, *yellow*, and *Colonial* — as anyone driving by might see it. But to make this story personal, Max needed to share what it was like for him living *inside* that house, as he did in his revision. When describing emotions, it works the same way. All your feelings come from inside you, but I see a lot of students earnestly attempting to show, not tell, emotions by describing them as if someone else were watching from the outside. They write sentences like the following, which also appeared in Max's first draft:

> I was happy in Massachusetts. The outside corners of my lips curved upward in a smile each time I experienced something new.

I read that, and I was like, "You managed to time travel all the way back to when you were four years old, swept away from an orphanage into an exciting new adventure in America, and *this* is what you remember?"

I think not. It's impossible to see yourself from outside yourself. That upward curve of the edges of lips reflected what someone else might have seen as he watched Max formulate a smile in slow motion. This kind of step-by-step, self-conscious description reads more like comprehensive instructions for how to make a smiley face than a description of Max's happiness at this pivotal time in his life.

When I pointed this out, Max could see how his description sounded fake. "But how am I supposed to remember details from when I was four years old?" Max asked.

That is such a legitimate question. Memories are fickle, and time alters them. Recounting memories is not an exact science, but recording what your mind chooses to remember, the essence of what happened, the feelings attached to the flashes of memory that appear to you when you believe you can time travel — those details result in writing that's the real deal. When Max became a true believer that he could manipulate his mind to time travel, he fully embodied his four-year-old self and wrote this:

> The day I left the orphanage with my parents and sister began an era of "first times." It was my first time riding in a car, in an elevator, on an escalator, in an airplane, and landing in New York City. Wow!

It only took a couple of sentences for me to *feel* Max's happiness and excitement and become excited *for* him. As I've said, the enthusiasm conveyed through good writing is contagious. You can read Max's completed essay in the Appendix, where you can also read Tyler's finished essay. (Do you remember Tyler from the Introduction?) Tyler's version of *firsts* shared as much about his distinct personality as Max's did.

> I will never forget what I am about to do because I'll only get my first ice hockey start once. I remember publishing my first article in the newspaper, my first race that I ever ran, and the first girl I ever kissed. I am hoping this will go a little bit better than all three of those firsts.

As you revise, remember that this is a *personal* essay you're sharing from your own, first-person point of view. If you were standing at a podium public speaking, you could feel your face heating up and the tickle of sweat beads dripping down your cheek, but you could not see that sweat glistening on your own bright-red forehead.

Traverse the Dimensions of Time and Space (aka Show, Don't Tell)

The bloodbath over, the battle won, your bizarre Frankenstein's monster of an essay draft might look a little anemic, like a shrunken head bobbling on a skeleton's body. In this chapter, you'll feed, fatten, and decorate your essay to look a little more human, more like you. The most fun and effective way to do that IMHO is to time travel back to the scene you're describing and *show* it, as Max learned to do.

The novelist E. L. Doctorow said, "Good writing is supposed to evoke sensation in the reader — not the fact that it is raining, but the feeling of being rained upon."

Another writer, Anton Chekhov, famously said, "Don't tell me the moon is shining; show me the glint of light on broken glass."

Every writer seems to have a different way to describe the concept of *show, don't tell*. I've contributed my own renditions of the *show, don't tell* philosophy throughout this book when I've suggested you time travel, don't fake it; write in scenes, not voice-overs; record specific details, not a generic summary; include readers, don't explain to them; and so on. Pick any version that speaks to you and run with it as you enhance your essay in this chapter.

The point of *show, don't tell* in your college essay is to conjure a moment so vividly that readers feel like you've invited them into your life for an intimate visit. This leads to engagement, which leads to a deeper understanding of you, which leads to the college application evaluator feeling like she knows you, which will compel her to fight for you in the admissions committee (despite that dip in your math grade sophomore year).

Use Your Common Senses

Show, don't tell is not limited to visuals. Use all your senses for inspiration as you add juicy details or substitute specific descriptions for generic ones.

What You See

- ***Time travel to a memory and hang out there.*** Close your eyes to see your past more clearly. Fully immerse yourself in the scene you're describing and notice what you're noticing. In the woods, I might notice decaying tree trunks, while you might notice the mushrooms growing on them. What you notice says something personal about you.
- ***Snap a mental photograph.*** Freeze a moment like a photograph and describe what you see in such ridiculous detail the reader can't help but paint a mental picture.

What You Hear

- ***Try dialogue*** in your essay. Please don't fixate on trying to remember the exact words someone said five years ago. The gist of them is also true.
- ***Substitute strong verbs for meh ones*** to make the sounds in your essay come alive, like Lia did when she wrote, "The marsh grass *crackled* in the wind. The waves *slapped* arrhythmically onto the shore."

What You Taste

Try going a step beyond words that describe the sensation of taste (sour, sweet, salty, bitter, umami — I love that word) to explore what the taste in your mouth reminded you of. *Fresh parsley made pasta primavera taste like Grandma's summer garden.*

What You Smell

To quote Levi, "The unmistakable skunky odor of red fox urine." Need I say more?

What You Feel on Your Body

- ***Evoke the sensation.*** Did it feel silky, jagged, fiery, freezing? Did it stab you? Did it tickle?
- ***Try a simile or metaphor***, a comparison with or without using the words *like* or *as*. Sonia wrote: "My arms lift round like a ballerina to hold a beach ball of energy."

What You Feel Emotionally

- ***Replace generic words for feelings*** that *explain* emotions (*sad, happy, nervous*) with specific words that *show* how it really looked, smelled, sounded, tasted, and felt in the moment. We're talking *eyes stinging* for *sad*, or *heart pumping* for *excited*. "I felt nervous" distances the reader. "The paper rattled in my hand" helps readers feel your jitters.
- ***Ask, "How do you know?"*** Here's a trick to help you *show* feelings. Try replacing *She felt good* (or *bad*) with a vivid, specific answer to *How do you know?* We know Mary felt happy at the end of Stevie's essay because "The smile on Mary's face lit up the room as she ceremoniously placed the hat on her head."

The Long and Short of It

Sometimes *showing* more specific, sensory details takes more words than *telling*. That's fine in draft 2, where content remains more important than correctness. Please don't consume yourself with how long and fat your essay becomes in the exercises in this chapter. Expect these middle drafts to yo-yo from skinny to fat and back again. Worrying about word count and other practicalities right now is premature, Inner Troll smack talk, and no fun (but enhancing your essay can be loads of fun).

Invite Awesomeness

Brain Booster

Now for a brief pause as both a warm-up for time travel and an elixir for mental health.

Instructions

1. **Go outside without your phone** and walk or just hang out.
2. **Notice** how insanely tall trees are.
3. **Notice** all the life teeming around you, even if you're on a seemingly empty street.
4. **Notice what you're noticing,** what you see, hear, smell, taste, and feel, and what you're thinking.
5. **When you've recognized the awesomeness** of nature and the world around you, you can go back inside and either add to your gratitude journal or dive right back into your essay revisions.

Surrounding yourself in nature relaxes the brain and invigorates the senses. You are now ready for some interior decorating.

Feed and Decorate

Writing Exercise

Instructions

1. **Read through your essay draft** looking for places to enhance it. Follow your remaining highlights to help you locate opportunities to add or substitute evocative details.
2. **When you find a worthy moment,** mentally travel back in time to the memory you're describing. When you land inside the past moment — when you can see, hear, smell, taste, and deeply feel it — *add* vivid sensory and emotional descriptions to your essay wherever opportunities arise. (Err on the side of "more is better" in this draft.)
3. **While you're in the moment,** *substitute* specific details for any vague or generic descriptions, explanations, or words that anyone could have written. Replace with abandon.

Helpful Hints

- If you can picture it in your mind, hear, smell, taste, or feel what you've written, leave those bits as they are or plump them up even more.
- If you highlighted information you thought you needed during the Hunt for Treasure exercise, but it sounds like a lecture when you read it out loud, you're probably *telling*. You can substitute *show*ier words for those didactic ones. We readers much prefer feeling like we're experiencing each moment for ourselves, and coming to our own conclusions, to being told what to think.

Dive Deep

What Is Your Essay Really *About?*

I've shared with you that the most successful personal essays have a narrative *and* a theme. Max wrote about his adoption. But his essay was really about personality characteristics developed in childhood that motivated everything he did. Sonia wrote about archery and gardening. But her essay was really about the connection between those two activities, both special, meditative escapes that sustained her. Evelyn wrote about her solo camping experience. But her essay was really about the perspective shift she brought home with her from that trip and applied to her life-in-progress.

You may already have had an *aha* moment about what your essay is really about when you wrote your first draft, but for most of us, understanding our essay's deeper layers is a four-draft process. You may never have thought about why you are the way you are before now, or your thoughts may have morphed since the last time you checked. Each essay draft provides another chance to contemplate some big questions about yourself. You don't need to reveal your deepest, darkest secrets in your college essay, but you don't have to pretend you have everything figured out either. Think of self-revelation in your writing as a service to others; connection is the goal. People feel less alone in the presence of a genuine, honest, sometimes vulnerable person.

When Show, Don't Tell *Flies Out the Window*

What is the meaning of my life?
Why am I the way I am?

The big philosophical questions require some abstract thinking, and personal insight is not easily shown. Telling has its place when you're attempting to communicate deeper reflection. Don't shy away from telling the reader your abstract thoughts, but do stick to showing vivid details and engaging readers with your descriptions throughout most of your essay.

Interrogate Your Essay

Writing Exercise

Interview your essay as if you're a journalist by using the five *W* and one *H* questions taught in journalism school. In this exercise, push beyond pretty additions and substitutions into the realm of *clear* and *meaningful*.

Instructions

Read through your essay, asking *Who?*, *What?*, *Where?*, *When?*, *Why?*, and *How?*, taking it one question at a time.

- **Who?** The answer is: You are the hero in this essay. Most sentences should begin with *I* (not *you* or *the team* or *everyone*). If lots of *we*s and *you*s appear as subjects of sentences, substituting *I* for some of them (and modifying the content accordingly) can make your essay instantly more personal.
- **What** is happening? If it's not clear, add or substitute information until it is, even if it takes more words. You may need to show the clarifying information in a descriptive sentence. As an example, *I was nervous as my audition began* becomes *My neck burned and voice quavered as my audition began*. Or sometimes a touch of telling illuminates what's happening more succinctly (but avoid expanding into a lengthy explanation).
- **Where** is the setting? Settings are fun to depict when you time travel and document sensory information

in the place where you landed. Showing the reader "a trail of glimmering white powder suspended in sunlight," as Levi did, includes and engages the reader in the essay's setting. Saying "The snow was pretty" does not.

- **When** did all this take place? Substituting or adding a couple of specific words should do the trick to clarify where you are in time. *A long time ago* becomes *three years ago* or *when I was six years old.*
- **Why** are you telling me all this? What is this essay really about? If you can't answer these questions, and the *point* of your essay is missing or lacking, try taking a few minutes to freewrite a paragraph reflecting more deeply about the meaning of your topic to you. Then try inserting what you discover (even if it's rough) into your essay.
- **How** do I know what is happening? Substitute specific descriptions for fuzzy, generic, unclear ones. Anyone could write a cliché like *feeling blue*. Only you can escort readers into your mind, so they can experience what feeling blue felt like to you.

Your draft is pleasantly plump! Don't freak out if your essay still does not look pretty. Draft 2 is done, and you're halfway there.

Part IV

DRAFT 3 — SWEAT THE SMALLER STUFF

Chapter 10

Sculpt Sentences

Shades of Blue

Look what you've done! You've made it through two whole drafts. (I'm clapping with delight.)

This is the part of the writing process when my student Sonia (who you've already met) asked me for reassurance on endless details in her essay.

"Does this sound good?"

"Do I need all this here?"

"Does this make sense?"

Finally, she threw up her hands and said, "I don't know what's wrong, but this part doesn't feel right."

I empathized with Sonia. The smallest decisions are often the hardest to make. It was easy for me to choose blue versus green paint for my bathroom walls. But my Inner Troll went bonkers scrutinizing the subtle variations of the 452 blue Benjamin Moore paint hues. *Would cool look better than warm? Would dark, light, gray-blue, or dusty blue make the room more inviting? Or is soothing the effect I should go for in a bathroom?* Clearly I did not want to paint my bathroom Old Pickup Blue or Varsity Blues (in my line of work). But how could I go wrong with Heaven on Earth or Serenity or Mystical Blue?

My husband looked at the square paint swatches stuck to the bathroom wall and said, "This is ridiculous. They all look the same."

By the second week of staring at those swatches, I had to acknowledge he was right. And I had déjà vu. I had gone through this exact same *inefficient* process when we'd painted the primary bath (Nantucket Fog) and the dining room (Wheatfield). And — just being honest with myself here — I had gone through similar agony figuring out the menu for every single dinner party I'd ever hosted (Blue or Gorgonzola cheese on the salad? Chicken thighs with or without skin? Snow or snap peas for a veggie side?).

Sweating the small stuff when making decisions was a theme in my life. It was time to paint the damn bathroom and move on. So I painted the bathroom Breath of Fresh Air blue, which sounded to me hopeful but also funny (because it was a bathroom), and here's what happened: *nothing*. No one ever paid attention to the bathroom walls again, not even me. Any of those blue paint colors would've been fine.

If you are my perfectionist compatriot, I'm here to give you a friendly little nudge in the forward direction. I derived no extra benefit from losing two weeks of my life to choosing a paint color, and you won't earn extra credit for spending two hours on a sentence.

Welcome to draft 3, where we sweat the smaller stuff (but not too much). In this chapter, we'll tackle some intangible elements of your essay that might not *feel* right, such as flow, tone, temperature, rhythm, size, and pace. We'll figure out the problem and how to solve it efficiently. When it comes to *shades of blue* decisions, like some of the ones you'll make in draft 3, a little fiddling can work wonders when your gut tells you something isn't right (you should always listen to your gut). But stressing over rewriting one sentence forty times is not fiddling. It's obsessing. "Clear, specific, succinct, done" is the draft 3 mantra I gifted to Sonia, and I pass this mantra on to you, along with the following sanity-saving exercise.

Body Scan

Brain Booster

Directing your mind toward your physical body is one way to interrupt *analysis paralysis* (because more thinking is not the solution for overthinking).

Instructions

1. **Assume a comfortable position.** Some more advanced yogis use special stools or sit cross legged. I (very much the amateur) lie flat on the ground, arms by my side, in the corpse position (Savasana).
2. **Minimize distractions.** Find the quietest place available to you. Lying still and closing one's eyes works well for tuning out the world.
3. **Settle in with a few deep breaths.** Inhale. Exhale. Inhale. Exhale. Inhale. Exhale.
4. **Slowly do a mental scan down your body.** Start with your head — awareness of your scalp, forehead, nose, cheeks, ears, mouth, chin. (No judgments about said head.) Shift your attention downward through your neck, shoulders, chest, arms, belly, thighs, knees, shins, ankles, and all the way down to your toes. Wherever you feel tension or tightness, try to let it go. If it remains, no problem. Continue your scan.
5. **Take slow, deep breaths as you open your eyes** and reenter your surroundings, ready to start fresh on your draft 3 revision excursion.

Go with the Flow

Keep that relaxed but refreshed body scan buzz going as I answer some questions students frequently ask about how to fix awkward parts of their essays.

Flow

Does this part feel smooth?

In draft 2, your essay underwent all sorts of contortions. You *moved, removed, added*, and *substituted* to the point that your essay may lurch from one (very good) idea to another (also very good) idea without a clear or fluid connection between them. If so, in draft 3 you can wedge *transitions* into the spaces between ideas. Sometimes you'll need to insert an entire sentence to improve the flow, though more often, a single word or a short phrase is enough.

Caution: Many students are tempted to begin a sentence with *And* or *But* to smooth a transition succinctly. You can do so sparingly, but overuse of *And* to begin a sentence can start to sound like you're cribbing the Bible. "And God said: 'Let there be light.' And there was light. And God saw the light..." And you can see why overusing *And* to begin sentences doesn't work out so well.

Does this transition seem awkward?

The goal for a transition is to move along from one idea to the next without drawing attention to the shifts. Maybe substituting a quick, casual transition word or phrase for a stuffier one is all that's required to smooth out the flow. If *on the contrary* feels jarring in the middle of a casual essay, substitute *instead of*. Scratch the transition *subsequent to the aforementioned events* and insert *an hour later* in its place. As another practical option, cut out the awkward transition altogether. Maybe you don't need it. *Maybe it's not a problem.* "Clear, specific, succinct, done."

Clarity

Does this part make sense?

Sometimes it only takes substituting specific word choices for vague ones to make ~~something~~ a murky sentence clear. Sometimes it takes ~~some telling instead of showing~~ a brief explanation to make sure ~~everything~~ a term or the chronology is clear, but it usually takes many fewer words than students think it will.

Can you tell where you are in my story?

Have you ever read a book and thought, *Wait, how old was she?* or *Was this before or after the part I just read?* When readers feel lost, it pops them out of the story. We want your readers to stay immersed.

In the name of clarity, instead of saying *later*, you can clarify for your reader how much later (*three years later*) so they won't feel lost or confused. Simple, succinct transitional words or phrases can clarify your timeframe: *When I was in eighth grade…then in tenth grade.* (You can chop out that entire paragraph of context summarizing everything that happened between eighth and tenth grade, if you haven't already.)

Rhythm

Does my essay feel stiff, like my energy and personality from draft 1 are gone?

I meant it when I told you in chapter 8 that your essay would become uglier before it matured into a show-stopping beauty. After so much manipulation, it makes sense if the language in draft 2 feels stilted. To resurrect the rhythm of your natural voice, read your essay out loud. Even if you feel silly, shut the door and do it. As you read, substitute words and phrases you'd really say, here and there, to loosen up the language until your natural voice returns to the page and your true personality reappears along with it. As an example, if you've never actually said the word *utilized* in a sentence, this is not the time or place to start.

Pace

Does my essay ramble on too long in certain parts or feel rushed in others?

If the pace feels off, your proportions are probably out of whack. Return to the trusty snowman shape as a loose guide: one-third beginning, one-third middle, one-third ending. Try shrinking or expanding sections of your essay. Cut some of the anecdote from the beginning if it takes up half the essay and leaves little space for reflections. Expand the third you skimped on with details, another example, or a thoughtful riff. Let go of an example (even a good one) if the middle drags on too long.

How can I identify where I over-*tell* and under-*show*?

The answer involves my family's first time playing the board game Catan. My eleven-year-old (at the time) son, the only experienced player among us, explained, "If you are red," he looked at me; I always choose red, "you can start by building two roads and two settlements. Then you draw your brick, wool, ore, or grain resource cards, but you hide them in your hand and roll the dice to see which terrain hexes…"

My mind wandered away from this onslaught of information I couldn't keep track of to the salted caramel ice cream in the freezer.

"Can we just play the game?" said my mind-reading daughter.

My son stopped talking. He rolled the dice, and the fun and whole point of family game night (playing the game together) began. The game moved right along. My son *showed* us the basics as we developed the island of Catan, drawing cards, building settlements and roads, collecting resources, and laughing, until my son announced, "I'll trade four of my lumber for one ore."

The game play stopped only long enough for my son to explain, "You can trade for whatever resource you need when it's your turn."

The purpose of explaining (telling) on game night or in a personal essay is to convey just enough necessary information to give your audience clarity, so they can return to the fun, most engaging part of your essay (showing). "Clear, specific, succinct, done" when it comes to *telling*, or you may lose your reader's attention to the salted caramel ice cream in the freezer.

Temperature

Is this funny or too much?

Turn up or down the spigot to control the temperature of your writing. The basic principle is to write *cold*, like a reporter documenting an unbiased news story, to avoid melodrama if your topic is already dramatic. Write *hot*, like the tiniest thing is the biggest deal in the world, to add drama or humor.

How do I write cold to avoid melodrama?

Remember Max who spent the first four years of his life in a Russian orphanage? His story was already dramatic, so he wrote the cold, hard, specific facts about his toddler life in the orphanage.

> Ten groups, ten kids in each, two caretakers per group, ten blue potty seats, ten tiny toothbrushes, ten toddler-sized

> beds. Awake time, meal time, bathroom time, play time, sleep time. Everything precise.

You can picture it. He invites you to feel for yourself the life of a little boy in this situation, without overdoing it with sentimental hardship adjectives (*freezing, harsh, decrepit, overcrowded*) to manipulate emotions and tell the reader how to feel. If your serious topic is in danger of mutating into melodrama, you can channel an impartial newspaper reporter and tone down or cut out altogether words that feel over-the-top.

How do I write hot for humor or dramatic effect?

Lots of students enter college hoping to become a doctor one day, but Emilio's essay reveals his *personal* approach to medicine (and everything else).

> I walked seemingly forever (really about forty steps) through the lobby, down the hallway, and to the surgery room, where I stood hugging the 100-pound pig tight. Everything seemed in slow motion as workers threw blankets and towels on the table, prepped the anesthesia machine and oxygen tanks, and set up the surgical instruments. I used extreme focus, like I would on a calculus test or watching the baseball strike my bat, to steady the pig who continued to scream and squirm as I lowered her onto the table where a couple of workers and I held her down until the anesthesia knocked her out.

All Emilio did was carry an animal, big drama for a small event, but the message was *No task is too small for Emilio to give it his all.* I can imagine any professor would want this guy in their class. You can read Emilo's essay in the Appendix and decide if you think the generous scholarship he received from the college of his choice was warranted. If you're going for humor or emphasis, you can pump up the volume for a hotter take on a lukewarm scene that's falling flat.

Why are you telling me all this about temperature?

Personal essay novices, earnestly attempting to *notice what they're noticing* and record it in copious, specific detail, can unintentionally write hot. The result becomes hyperaware sentences, written self-consciously, as if in slow motion, like Max's methodical description "the outside corners of my lips curved upward in a smile." Making a big, dramatic thing out of a mundane moment can be funny or highlight a message, as in Emilio's essay. But if drama is not what the writer was going for — it wasn't for Max — writing hot could come off as a bit of a cringer. On the other hand, writing cold can inadvertently materialize as a factual summary and read like an instruction manual and a yawner. You have the power to dial up or down your essay's temperature until you reach the effect you intended.

Size

What should I cut if my essay is still way, way (way) too long?

We've ignored size in favor of beauty, but it's time to start making some choices. If your essay draft is far too long, look for the following opportunities to chop it down to closer to 650 words.

- Did you say almost the same thing in two separate sentences? *Solution:* Pick one and cut the other.
- Did you write a lengthy explanation that goes on too long? *Solution:* Cut words to make the description shorter and more specific, or substitute a less wordy clarification.

- Did you veer off on a tangent that no longer serves your essay? *Solution:* Slice it away.
- Did you include multiple examples to show your point? *Solution:* If your essay is running long, remove one or more of those examples.
- Did you repeat yourself unnecessarily or use weak or passive verbs you could eliminate? *Solution:* You can look forward to solving both of these problems, the two most common mechanical culprits that add unnecessary length, in chapter 11.

Caution: I beg you, please don't give up showing for telling for the sake of length.

Do I Sound Likable? (It's a Tone Thing.)

Of course, you *are* likable. Let's make sure the tone of your essay reflects your appeal. Up until draft 3, we've focused on saying what you want to say. I *do* want you to feel like you've truly expressed yourself in your essay, but now we must think about the effect your words will have on readers, to help them interpret what you want to say in the way you hope they will understand it. Ask yourself the following questions, and the answers might lead to some tone adjustments.

Would I like the writer of this essay?

Channel a well-intentioned stranger reading your essay. Would you want to invite the author to a party...or to live in your community or to become your college roommate? If not, which parts of your essay put you off or make you wince? You have the power to change or cut them.

Does any part of my essay sound like a social media profile?

Trying to project the image of an ideal student campaigning for admission to a college can give the impression of pandering. No matter how well you think you disguised it, selling yourself in any form in the context of a personal essay can sound either pompous or, conversely, a little desperate. If it presents as a humble bragging (or openly bragging), cut it or tone it down for humility's sake. Paste the boasting where it belongs, in the Activities or Honors section of your college application (nicknamed the *brag sheet*).

Do I sound overly competitive?

In the most important sporting event of your life, you score, you win, you reach the pinnacle of success. Laser focus on a positive outcome, regardless of how ruthless you had to act to accomplish it, creates a winner, right? Maybe — society loves a winner — but in a personal essay this emphasis on achievement can seem cutthroat.

The hard truth: People driven by results don't do as well in college admissions (or in life) as those driven by the experience itself, win or lose, whether the endeavor is athletic, intellectual, or creative. College admission readers find essays exploring how the student learned and grew from an experience much more attractive than essays focusing on the outcome.

Does the vocabulary in my essay sound natural?

Some well-read students have a large vocabulary that emerges instinctively as they write. You may be one of them. And a thesaurus can be a great tool if it reveals the correct word to say what you mean. However, using puffed-up academic language or résumé words (*demonstrated core competencies, facilitated*) to look impressive can give a pretentious or desperate-to-please vibe instead. Substitute natural language to bring the tone of your essay back down to earth.

Caution: Using words you don't normally use can go horribly wrong. Case in point, a failed revision I read with the sentence "College will withhold a symbiotic relationship with myself." Huh? A student really wrote this, luckily in draft 2, in time to correct the gaffe in draft 3.

Does too much explaining come across as condescending?

Clear is good, but the reader is smart and doesn't need as much explaining as you may think. The easy solution: Trim down the lengthy explanation of a word or concept to only the necessary information. Check out Priya's eight-word definition of the debate term *spreading*, "the combination of the words 'speed' and 'reading.'" This was a great feat of pruning, as her first draft included a two-paragraph *spreading* explanation.

Do I sound like a downer?

Consider three different ways to express math anxiety.

- I hate math.
- Math is totally useless.
- Math challenges me.

Which might a former math major evaluating your application in a college's office of admission find most appealing? Which do *you* find most appealing? If any bit of your essay sounds too negative or judgmental, tweak the word choice until the tone sounds more optimistic or open-minded.

Could my description of the obstacle I faced make me sound like a complainer?

You might have faced a horror show and have the right to complain. But wallowing at length in the unfairness, injustice, or bad luck that caused the problem could sound whiny. Blaming (a bad teacher, controlling parents, an unfair rule) has even less allure than fixating on the problem. You can shift the focus away from the culprit and back to you by limiting your description of the obstacle to the first third of your essay. Then switch gears. How did you bounce back, learn a valuable lesson, and handle yourself in the aftermath? Your perseverance is the real story here.

Could my writing about mental or physical health issues come across as worrisome?

If you've suffered from a concussion, torn ACL, prolonged illness, anxiety, or depression, you are far from alone. Admission evaluators (who are human beings, after all) will feel compassion. But if your whole essay describes what's plaguing you, they might also feel concerned that the college cannot accommodate your needs.

Spend at least two-thirds of the essay space on the ways your struggles have contributed to your growth, even if overcoming them is a work-in-progress (join the club). Readers will feel empathy and reassurance, rather than hesitation about your ability to thrive in college. See Melanie's essay in the Appendix as an example of effectively addressing the theme of struggles with anxiety.

Did I steer clear of anything that might make me look vulnerable?

While spending the entire essay space describing your difficulties is not recommended, vulnerabilities are part of the human condition. Nobody is perfect, so painting yourself as a person with zero weaknesses in your essay can feel disingenuous and unrelatable to your imperfect reader. Acknowledging vulnerability adds dimension to your character and can help draw readers in.

Does my essay make me seem like a recluse when I'm really a people person?

Art can be a solo endeavor, but Cassidy was extremely social, and her essay showcased both sides of her. Even Levi's essay about a quiet, outdoor experience alone included other people when he gave a nod to his rock-climbing teammates, as well as campers and a mentor at his wilderness summer camp. If your essay feels lonely, consider populating it with others (using small brushstrokes) to show readers you'll cohabitate well with future roommates and contribute to future college classrooms.

Does my essay skimp on self-reflection?

Without deeper reflection about why your topic matters to you, readers may not comprehend how intellectually capable you really are. They might wonder about your ability to handle the depth of analysis required in college-level academics, despite your excellent high school grades. Every essay draft offers another chance to reflect more deeply, and this is the moment in draft 3.

Have any of your answers to the Down the Reflection Rabbit Hole exercise in chapter 3 changed or crystallized? This would be a good time to return to the warren and revisit them. I'll also pose some new big (maybe unanswerable, though thought-provoking) questions, which may help you add a layer of depth.

- How did you grow and change between the beginning of your essay-in-progress and the end?
- When did not knowing something hinder you in the past?
- How has knowing what you know now made your life (so far) better?
- How will you use the knowledge you've accumulated in your future endeavors?
- What do you want anyone reading this essay to understand about you?

- Why are you the way you are?
- What do you share in this essay that helped shape you into today's version of yourself?

Freewrite on any of these questions that stand out to you (try setting a ten-minute timer and digging in). Slip any new insights into your essay. Note that sometimes adding or substituting one sentence of deeper insight is enough to elevate an essay's effectiveness.

Do I sound privileged when writing about my service to people "less fortunate" than me?

How wonderful that you're excited enough about serving others to write about it in your college essay. Double-check that your language doesn't imply superiority over those you are serving. If you've compared yourself with any group that is "less fortunate" or "underprivileged," you can inadvertently feed into the perception of tone deafness about your own privilege.

The solutions are specificity and empathy. Try to substitute a specific human being for the generic "less fortunate" or "underserved" group. What do you have in common with this person you are serving? What qualities do you see in them that you see in yourself? Check out Cassidy's and Stevie's essays for examples of service project topics handled with specificity and empathy.

Could anything in my essay offend someone?

Of course you don't mean to offend anyone. If you suspect something you wrote could be off-putting, it's best to cut it out altogether or at least soften the tone. If you're not sure, don't fret. You can ask your trusty proofreaders to help you catch any unintentional offenses in chapter 13.

Tinker

Writing Exercise

As you pull together all the sculpting tools you've collected and apply them to your essay, please keep in mind that tinkering does not mean second-guessing every sentence. Use "Done is better than perfect" as a mantra if playing with sentences becomes prolonged or frustrating. (Setting a timer to limit yourself to thirty minutes will also help.)

Instructions

Make subtle revisions to improve flow, clarity, rhythm, pace, temperature, size, and tone.

Helpful Hints

- **Smooth transitions** between ideas with as few words as possible.
- **Clarify** anything that remains cloudy.
- **Read aloud** and infuse your personality into the rhythm so the language sounds like you.
- **Pace yourself** and fix the one-third of your essay that feels too long (make cuts) or too short (add compelling details).
- **Adjust to room temperature** by cooling down descriptions for serious moments or heating them up for humor or dramatic effect.
- **Trim** long explanations and use the extra space to reflect more deeply.
- **Replace** stuffy, formal words and phrases with more casual, conversational ones.
- **Cut** humble bragging or blatantly bragging and potential offenses.

Matching Start to Finish

In the next writing exercise, you'll revisit your beginning and ending for more fiddling fun. But before you do, for kicks and giggles (and maybe a burst of clarity or inspiration), let's look at the matchmaking of beginnings and endings written by real students in their essays from the Appendix.

Levi

Beginning: Snow tracking is hard. The prints aren't completely clear, but I can still make out the little X of negative space formed between foot pads.

Ending: This was the human experience for thousands of years before TV and social media. We were part of that rhythm. It's grounding returning to it. It's my reboot.

Levi begins with a wildlife tracking scene and ends with why tracking is meaningful to him.

Stevie

Beginning: The first "hat" I knitted was a twisted mess, too large for any head, far from something wearable.

Ending: The smile on Mary's face lit up the room as she ceremoniously placed the hat on her head. Like my first hat, hers didn't fit right, and the pattern looked a little lopsided, but it was a beautiful hat, we all agreed.

Stevie begins with learning to knit and ends with teaching others to knit.

Max

Beginning: Structured, organized, disciplined; these are not qualities one would generally use to describe a toddler.

Ending: Structured, organized, disciplined; these are not qualities one would generally use to describe a teenager, but all along, they've described me.

Max starts with qualities that defined him as a little kid and ends with the way those special characteristics still define him now.

Melanie

Beginning: My life goal (even if I don't pursue it until I'm eighty-five) is to build myself a functional, maximum-500-square-foot tiny house that I can haul across the nation to see all the national parks and experience every state, including Alaska.

Ending: In the Grand Canyon, I started building its foundation.

Melanie starts with a dream and ends with progress toward making that dream reality.

Beginning and Conclusion Collusion

Writing Exercise

Instructions

Play with your beginning and ending until you feel confident answering the following questions in the affirmative. (If you have perfectionist tendencies, set a timer for twenty minutes to complete this one. We still have another essay draft to go.)

First, return to the place it all began, by which I mean your beginning.

- Do the first sentence and first paragraph capture your attention?

- Clear is more important than catchy. Is it clear where you are in time and space?
- Would you keep reading after the first paragraph of your essay?

Now skip down to your ending.

- Is it clear what you're trying to say?
- Is your ending compatible with the beginning of your essay?
- What does that last paragraph reveal about you?
- Does it feel like a finale?
- Does your ending leave the reader with a better understanding of who you are as a human being than they had at the beginning?

Beautification in progress! If you're itching to *get this right*, the next chapter is your happy place.

Chapter 11

Fix

My student Stevie was a creative genius. They could act, sing, weave, sew, knit, bead, and crochet gifts that would wow you (and win you over as a friend for life). Stevie wrote an impassioned first draft…riddled with mistakes. Once their essay's content satisfied them, the mission of correcting those errors began. With their accumulation of grammar and syntax knowledge came the independence to recognize basic mistakes in *all* their writing and the understanding of how to fix them.

I am now 100 percent invested in *your* writing competency. It's (drumroll) *finally* time for fixing. No more tackling intangibles. You'll right that which is wrong in this chapter where run-on sentences and fragments will vanish and verbs will become a magical elixir. We now shift our attention from the artful manipulations we performed in chapter 10 that massaged the feel of the essay to outright editing for correctness. You have entered your Inner Editor's playground. (Perfectionists rejoice!)

Caution: Your helpful Inner Editor, who fixes things, is not the same as your Inner Troll, who destroys confidence and everything else it touches.

I've met numerous straight-A students who had never heard of passive voice, had never thought about weak verbs at all, and didn't realize they wrote run-on sentences until I pointed them out. No shame for any grammar mistakes you didn't know you were making before this chapter. One of the goals of the application essay you're writing is to "demonstrate writing competency." So let's demonstrate the hell out of your competency to college admission evaluators and at the same time develop some grammar skills that will empower you and make your future professors want to hug you for the clean, error-free papers you hand in. Consider this chapter, which deals with *sentence-level* revisions, as a gateway to draft 4, where you'll nitpick word by word.

How Facebook Saved My Family

Fun fact: Run-on sentences are the most common grammar mistake (by far) in high school students' essays.

Today I recruit you to help stop the spread of run-ons and sentence fragments. See if you can find those grammatical mistakes in the following short lesson that proposes one good reason why social media is not all bad.

This Is a True Story (with Many Run-Ons and Sentence Fragment Mistakes)

> I avoided joining Facebook like I avoid the guy with a wet cough in the grocery aisle. Until one day my husband (who has granted permission for me to publicize this event for the common good) was in the bathroom. He saw the cardboard toilet paper roll hung from its holder without a square of toilet paper coiled around it.
>
> No, he did not use a towel, he yelled for the only other person in the house, our daughter. No footsteps creaked down the hallway to rescue him. He whipped out his iPhone. Which is always attached to him like an extra limb. His phone rang and rang, our daughter didn't pick up. He texted her, nothing, he was 99% sure our daughter was online checking her Facebook feed (this was early social media, pre-Instagram) while he suffered in the primary bath. My husband snapped a photo of the empty

cardboard roll, he direct-messaged her the photo and wrote, "TP pleeeease?!!!!" he waited.

Footsteps creaked down the hallway. A gleaming white roll of toilet paper appeared. Through a crack in the bathroom door. Because of Facebook, my husband suffered no more, I finally joined Facebook to save my family in the event of another emergency. If you friend me on Facebook. I can save you too.

How to Check If It's a Complete Sentence

I'm sure you learned this in elementary school, but let's review to set the groundwork to eradicate those pesky run-ons and fragments from your life for good. To identify a sentence, ask yourself these three questions:

1. Does the phrase have a *subject* (someone or something performing an action)?
2. Does it contain a *verb* (an action performed by the subject, or the state of being of the subject)?
3. Is it a *complete thought* that makes sense on its own?

If you can answer yes to all three of these questions, you have found yourself a bona fide full sentence.

Start at the bottom of my story. We'll read upward from the last sentence to the first to eliminate context. When an isolated phrase dangles before you, you can more easily see if it makes sense on its own when you read it out loud.

I can save you too.

The last sentence in my small family saga has a subject (*I*) and a verb (*can save*), and it makes sense on its own. It's a full sentence! No corrections needed.

Next, read the second-to-last sentence in my family drama.

If you friend me on Facebook.

Does this sound right to you? Something is missing. If you friend me on Facebook, then what will happen? This is not a complete thought on its own. It needs help to make sense. We've found our first sentence fragment!

How to Fix a Sentence Fragment

- ***Repair 1 (recommended): Attach it to a complete sentence*** standing right beside it.

  If you friend me on Facebook, I can save you too.

- ***Repair 2: Add whatever is missing*** to finish the sentence so it can stand alone.

  If you friend me on Facebook, I can help you in a pickle.

- ***Repair 3: Subtract the culprit.*** In this case, the dependent word *if* is the problem.

  Friend me on Facebook.

Fun fact: In the command (aka imperative) form, the subject of the sentence in repair 3 is an implied *you*. That's why the correction stands alone as a legitimate sentence.

How to Find a Run-On Sentence

Next, read aloud the third-to-last sentence.

> Because of Facebook, my husband suffered no more, I finally joined Facebook to save my family in the event of another emergency.

There's something wrong with this sentence as it's written. Can you feel it? It's muddled and runs on and on (a clue). Start again to read the sentence out loud. When you reach the first comma, stop.

> Because of Facebook,

Does this phrase have a subject? (Facebook could be a subject, since it's a noun.) A verb? (It does not.) Does it make sense on its own? (No sirree.) Start reading the sentence again and stop at the next comma.

> Because of Facebook, my husband suffered no more,

This is a full sentence that makes sense on its own, though it's not punctuated correctly (yet). *My husband* is the subject, and *suffered* is the verb.

Use your hand to cover the full sentence you just checked (another nifty technique to isolate phrases), and let's see what the rest *after* the comma looks like.

> I finally joined Facebook to save my family in the event of another emergency.

It's also a full sentence that makes sense on its own. *I* is the subject and *joined* is the verb.

This run-on third-to-last sentence in my story is actually two sentences!

The Comma Splice, an Especially Sneaky Style of Run-On Sentence Error

We have now encountered the most common and crafty kind of run-on called a *comma splice*. A comma alone is not strong enough to glue together two complete sentences that could make sense on their own. The tricks you performed, isolating the sentence parts separated by commas and reading each part aloud, will help you locate those wily comma splices.

How can we fix a comma splice? Let me count the ways. (There are four.)

- ***Repair 1 (recommended): Use a period*** instead of a comma to split it into two sentences.

  Because of Facebook, my husband suffered no more. I finally joined Facebook to save my family in the event of another emergency.

- ***Repair 2 (recommended every so often): Use a semicolon.*** A semicolon is weaker than the full stop of a period but stronger than a comma and strong enough to connect two closely associated full sentences. Semicolons tend to draw attention to themselves, so use them sparingly in your short essay.

  Because of Facebook, my husband suffered no more; I finally joined Facebook to save my family in the event of another emergency.

- ***Repair 3 (enthusiastically recommended): Add a conjunction,*** which is a suitable joining word. You can remember which little words are conjunctions because they are FANBOYS (*for*, *and*, *nor*, *but*, *or*, *yet*, *so*). A comma plus one of the FANBOYS is strong enough to glue two complete sentences together.

Because of Facebook, my husband suffered no more, so I finally joined Facebook to save my family in the event of another emergency.

- ***Repair 4 (not recommended but included for fun): Add a dependent word or phrase*** (such as *if, when, after which*) or subtract a subject or verb (or both) to make one of the complete sentences incomplete.

  Because of Facebook, my husband suffered no more, after which I finally joined Facebook to save my family in the event of another emergency.

Bonus challenge: Find and fix the rest of the run-on and sentence fragment errors in my "How Facebook Saved My Family" story. There are ten errors total — eleven if you count the unchanged empty toilet paper roll (it was not me).

Run-On Sentence and Fragment Repair Shop

Writing Exercise

Instructions

- **Read your essay aloud and backward** (sentence by sentence, from the last to the first) to find run-ons and sentence fragment mistakes.
- **When you find a run-on** sentence, a period or a comma plus *and* is usually the easiest way to fix it. A semicolon also works, or if you're feeling rowdy, try throwing in a dependent word like *when* or *as*.

- **When you find a sentence fragment**, either attach it to a complete thought or add the missing VIPs (very important parts) of the sentence.

Lights, Camera, Action Verbs

I become (perhaps disproportionately) excited about my favorite part of speech. *Verbs* have the magical power to resurrect a piece of writing from the dead. One powerful verb can enliven a sentence and change the entire picture you have in your mind, making that verb as descriptive as any adjective or adverb. Watch what happens to the image in your mind when I change only the verb in a simple sentence.

Joanne *went* to the store.
Joanne *skipped* to the store.
Joanne *limped* to the store.

Do you see what I mean? And get this — with an *-ing* ending, verbs can even become *nouns*. (How cool is that?!)

Crawling is Joanne's favorite way to travel to the store.

One of the greatest grammar and syntax-related gifts I can give you (and it will be my pleasure to do so) is the power to transform the verbs in *your* essay from weak to strong. Showing you how to find and strengthen the weak verbs in your writing is the next item on my bucket list.

*Start by Looking for the Awful A's (*Allow *and* Able*)*

Treat the words *allow* and *able* as archenemies and a signal of withering verb strength. When you see an *Awful A*, eradicate it and change the verb form to make the sentence active.

I was *able* to paint my room. (It sounds like an accident or a stroke of good fortune.)
I *painted* my room. (You deserve credit for your initiative and your work.)
Buying paint *allowed* me to paint my room. (The paint allowed nothing. Paint is inanimate. If we relied on the paint for permission, every room would have wallpaper.)
I *painted* my room. (That's more like it.)

To Be or Not to Be

Pay attention anywhere you used *being* or *to be* in those exact forms.

Replace these forms of *to be* with an action verb when possible. (It's not always possible, but often it is.)

I want to be an actor and dream of being on a Broadway stage.
I dream of acting on a Broadway stage.

Look for all the other forms of the verb to be — *is*, *am*, *are*, *was*, *were*, *be*, and *been*.

Especially when a bunch of little helping verbs show up in a cluster, assess whether you can substitute one strong, active verb for all those piddly ones.

Li *was going to be* a farmer, but now she *is going to be* a lawyer.
Li *chose* law over farming.

Let's give a special shout-out to *There is* (also *there are*, *was*, and *were*), which often dooms a sentence to weakness from the start.

There were no mistakes left in draft 3.
The writer obliterated the mistakes in draft 3.

I am not suggesting you change every single sentence with a

form of *to be* in it. We English speakers use *to be* variations often in casual conversation, and we want your essay to feel authentic. Aim for 80 percent elimination of *to be* verbs (preview of the Brain Booster coming up). Or if that sounds outrageous, pick a percentage that seems reasonable to you. Eliminating just 20 percent will still strengthen your essay.

Look for Vague Little Throwaway Verbs

When you see vague verbs like *have* or *get*, see if you can find a more specific verb to add meaning to your sentence.

> Luca *got* his school lunch. (This doesn't say much.)
> Luca *stole* his school lunch. (This verb says something personal about Luca, for better or worse.)

Catch Passive Voice

Passive voice happens when the subject of a sentence receives the action of the verb rather than performing the action. The real topic of your essay is you. Therefore, writing in passive voice *weakens* you as you sit back and are acted upon rather than taking initiative and doing the acting yourself. You are strong, so embrace your power to purge passive voice and write with confidence.

> The bathroom *was cleaned by me.* (Why is the bathroom the star of the sentence? The real star of this story is you, the one down on your hands and knees scrubbing.)
> *I cleaned* the bathroom. (Well done.)

Here's a fun trick to help you find passive voice. When you add the words *by clowns* to the end of your sentence, if it makes sense, it's passive voice.

The whole cake *was eaten* (by clowns).

Try adding the subject of the sentence to the beginning, followed by the simple, active form of the verb, and you'll have a stronger, cleaner sentence.

I ate the whole cake. (Or if you don't want anyone to know the cake-eater was you, try "*Clowns ate* the whole cake" as an alibi.)

The Fringe Benefits, Beyond Correctness, of Strengthening Your Verbs

Here's an example of verb strengthening done right.

Draft 1: I should have been able to work harder instead of wasting all that time being a procrastinator.

Draft 3: I wasted time procrastinating instead of working hard.

Watch out for that trickster *able* and boring *being*, the culprits that make that sentence clunky in draft 1. Substituting snazzier verbs for blah ones in draft 3 makes everything clearer and revs up an essay's pace and energy. Plus, cutting out all those lifeless little helping verbs saves precious word space in your short essay. Win-win-win.

Caution: You will notice that throughout this book I break all sorts of my own grammar and syntax rules, including inserting forms of *to be* willy-nilly (though no *Awful A's* beyond examples in this chapter), in favor of capturing my genuine voice on the page. Strengthen verbs to tighten sentences when you can, while staying true to the sound of your own voice.

Now I can check *strengthening weak verbs* off my bucket list.

Aim for 80 Percent

Brain Booster

Before you release your Inner Editor to play with grammar, the Pareto Principle can provide some perspective. It goes like this: 80 percent of our results come from 20 percent of our effort. I promise you'll feel 80 percent happier if you don't spend another hour trying to make one sentence 20 percent better.

Instructions

If, after two hours, you notice darkness descending outside and you're still working on fixing that one sentence, *aim for 80 percent* and good enough. Then move on. Chances are your 80 percent is another person's 180 percent.

Strengthen the Weak

Writing Exercise

Instructions
Sift through your essay for the *Awful A's* (*able* and *allow*) and the *To Be*s (*to be*, *being*, *been*, *am*, *is*, *are*, *was*, and *were*). When you see weak verbs, try substituting stronger action verbs in their place.

Repeat Phrase Offenders

After I make one more point about verbs, it's time to move along to a few more of the most common grammar delinquents I often see in students' essays, so you can spot and correct them in your draft 3.

Misunderstandings and Outright Disagreements

When verbs disagree with each other in tense, or they disagree with their subject in number, chaos ensues. Don't even get me started on what happens when pronoun confusion joins the mix. Consistency and specificity resolve the resulting skirmishes.

> ***Draft 1:*** My alarm clock and my stomach conspires to wake me up at 4:00 a.m. I smacked the button to stop it from disrupting a delightful dream.

Pronoun Confusion

I have questions about that draft 1 sentence. To start, which "button" did you smack to stop what? Did you hit the snooze button to stop the alarm clock's beeping or your belly button to stop your stomach's growling?

Subject-Verb Agreement

Next question: *My alarm clock* and *my stomach* combine to form a compound subject. If both the alarm clock and your stomach conspired to disrupt your delightful dream, then why does the verb *conspires* appear in the singular?

Verb Tense Shifts

Finally, the verb *conspires* is in the present tense, but in the next sentence the verb *smacked* shifted to the past tense with an *-ed* ending. So was this unwelcome wake-up call a one-time annoyance that happened in the past, or does the buzzing and grumbling wake you up every morning?

> ***Draft 3:*** My alarm clock and my stomach conspired to wake me up at 4:00 a.m. I smacked the snooze button to stop the beeping alarm from disrupting a delightful dream.

The corrections in draft 3 answered all my questions. And if I were you, I'd eat a bigger dinner and double-check the settings on my alarm clock before bedtime to prevent a repeat. Sweet dreams.

The Crime of Repetition

Maybe it's not really a criminal act, but some might consider repetition a misdemeanor when it comes to this essay. You can combine and consolidate sentences when you see the same words repeating. It will save you word space in your essay and make it clearer.

Draft 1: We have two friendly neighborhood zombies. Their names are Sarah and Steve. Because Sarah and Steve are zombies, they will never die. Because they will never die, they are going to walk around the streets in our neighborhood forever. They walk with stiff legs because they are zombies.

These sentences are not incorrect per se, but a 650-word essay does not include space for all that repetition (and we prevented the zombie apocalypse when you shut off your phone back in chapter 2).

Draft 3: Sarah and Steve, our friendly neighborhood zombies, will walk stiff legged around the local streets forever.

Misplaced Modifiers

I saved my favorite common sentence structure mistake for last because it's the court jester of grammar errors.

Draft 1: The teacher handed out cookies to the children stored in a plastic container.

Obviously, it is never okay to store children in a plastic container.

Draft 3: The teacher handed out cookies stored in a plastic container to the children.

Luckily, moving the misplaced modifier (*stored in a plastic container*) closer to what it's describing (*cookies*) will prevent a lawsuit or worse.

Your Inner Editor's Fixing Funhouse

Writing Exercise

Let your Inner Editor loose to live its best life!

Instructions

1. **Find and fix common grammar mistakes** where they appear in your own essay.
2. **Continue to condense your essay,** if needed, with the tools you've collected in this chapter, inching closer to 650 words.

Helpful Hints

- **Strengthen the weak verbs** you may have missed, especially the ones with all those little space-sucking helping verbs such as *could have been* or *am able to be*.
- **Moderate any disagreements among verbs and pronouns.**
- **Slice out repetition** by cutting words that repeat and combining and consolidating sentences.
- **Choose the best parts of your essay and**

ruthlessly slash the rest. Even if you once loved them, sometimes you must "kill your darlings" in favor of succinctness. (In truth, your darlings will remain mummified in an earlier draft, just in case.)

Pat your Inner Editor on the back for a job well done! More (comma) drama and semi(colon)-madness coming right up in draft 4. Yes, you have made it all the way to draft 4 (the crowd goes wild).

Part V

DRAFT 4 — POLISH

Chapter 12

Fuss

The Sparkly Cleanup

Our friend and contractor, Rob, basically lived in our house during our home renovation. At the end of each day, Rob would say, "It's time for the sparkly cleanup." He would sweep away the sawdust so our whole family could gather and admire his day's work. After the renovation's completion, we threw a celebration dinner for Rob and his wife. When they left, my husband was the one who performed the sparkly cleanup (of dishes), but Rob deserves credit for the sparkly cleanup concept, which has stuck with me.

I welcome you to draft 4, your sparkly cleanup after your renovation work. Can you feel our focus shrinking? We looked at whole paragraphs in draft 2, fiddled with sentences in draft 3, and in draft 4, we'll fuss with individual words. Now we nitpick because errors can become a game changer *in the wrong direction* for a personal essay.

Thank you to AI for catching so many needless word-level mistakes like those typos you made when you were writing fast in your rough draft. While AI may have capitalized the stand-alone letter *I* for you and reversed the *i* and the *e* when you accidentally misspelled *believe*, you know from texting that autocorrect and spellcheck will miss (or even create) errors sometimes. We need flesh-and-blood human beings to add context and meaning to words so they come together correctly and as intended.

It has been a while since elementary school (for some of us, longer than others) when you learned capitalization, usage, punctuation, and spelling (CUPS) rules. Therefore, later in this chapter I bequeath to you a handy-dandy CUPS proofreading shortcut sheet to help with small but crucial corrections when AI fails you. Use it as an aid to eliminate all errors in your college application, your high school and college papers, office memos, your future novel or memoir, and your Academy Award acceptance speech. (Why not you?)

Caution: Your Inner Editor, livin' the dream in this chapter, might want everything just so. But your Inner Editor is your *assistant*, not a fascist dictator. You are the one in control. Take it from me; each sentence can become a daylong project if you let it.

Triple-Checking Tips and Tricks (to Use for This Essay and All Your Writing)

Tip 1: Sit (or sleep) on it like you did with draft 1. You can catch more mistakes if you leave your essay alone for a night, a week, or a month if you have the time, and then revisit it with fresh eyes.

Tip 2: Read aloud like you did when you found and fixed run-on sentences and sentence fragments. You'll trip over sentences that need correcting. You'll notice you've skipped over little words like *an* or *so*, or that you need a comma (or period) where you paused to take a breath.

Tip 3: Read it backward, which you also have practiced. Start with the last sentence, and read the whole essay, one sentence at a time, all the way up to the beginning. You'll isolate each sentence to make sure it's correct on its own.

Reading backward *and* out loud is especially effective for catching run-ons and fragments.

*Tip 4: **Proofread extra carefully wherever you made changes.*** Those are the most likely places typos will show up.

*Tip 5: **Recognize when enough is enough.*** If you find yourself fiddling with one sentence for half an hour, maybe it's good enough as is. *What if it's not a problem?* If you have the overdo-it gene, aim for 80 percent and don't panic about finding every tiny error because in the next chapter, your chosen readers will help you catch any lingering mistakes you've missed.

Take a Self-Compassion Break

Brain Booster

You deserve a little break before you jump into editing minutiae in your essay. While you take a breather, indulge in self-love with a variation on a method some psychologists use in therapy.

Instructions

1. **Close your eyes and hug yourself**, arms crossed in front of you, hands resting on upper arms.
2. **Now give yourself little pats** with your hands and rub your hands up and down your biceps.
3. **Keep tapping and massaging** your arms and hold the hug position until you feel super-relaxed and validated.

Now you can focus all that positive energy on your nitpicky edits.

CUPS Proofreading Shortcut Sheet (for Human Eyeballs When AI Lets You Down)

Capitalization: MINTS

- **M**onths (plus days of the week and holidays but not seasons)
- **I** (when it refers to yourself)
- **N**ames (of cities, countries, nationalities, languages, and people like *Mom* if it makes sense to substitute their name but not *my mom*)
- **T**itles (such as *College Essay Confidence*, as well as time periods like the Renaissance and events like the Super Bowl)
- **S**tarts of sentences and quotes

Usage

- Double negative = positive (I *didn't* do *nothing*! Ooh, a confession!).
- Cut most *-ly* words (avoid overusing adverbs).
- Pick and choose the best adjectives (avoid overdoing it with descriptors).
- Replace meaningless or generic words (*awesome, kind of, thing, get*) with specific words when possible.

Punctuation

- Comma: pause (it helps to read aloud and implant a comma when you pause for a breath)
- Semicolon: used like a period, but sparingly (or to separate longer phrases in a list)

- Colon: list or explanation to follow
- Period: full stop
- Parentheses: separate aside phrases or clauses from the rest of the sentence
- Quotation marks: surround words said out loud or emphasized
- Exclamation point (!): emphasizes strong emotion or surprise
- Ellipsis (…): words trail off or were omitted
- Apostrophe: missing letters (*I'll = I will*) or possession (Coco's cup)

Spelling: Some Commonly Confused or Misspelled Words with Model Sentences

- *They're* vs. *There* vs. *Their* (They're over there with their parents.)
- *Too* vs. *To* vs. *Two* (It's never too late to visit more than two ice cream shops.)
- *Let's* vs. *Lets* (Let's see if Mom lets us see the sea.)
- *Loose* vs. *Lose* (I lose my mind when my pocket is heavy with loose change.)
- *It's* vs. *Its* (Vatican City is capitalized because it's its own country.)
- *Affect* vs. *Effect* (Humidity affects my hair. The effect is crazy curls.)
- *Than* vs. *Then* (We'll visit two colleges, then compare which college offers more of what I want than the other.)
- *Accept* vs. *Except* (I accept all cookies except stale ones.)
- *A lot* is two words. So is *all right*. (*Alright* is not a real word, but it's used a lot.)

House of Corrections

Writing Exercise

Instructions

Have at the ready your CUPS Proofreading Shortcut Sheet and additional tips.

- Read aloud, backward, or upside down — in whatever way helps you catch pesky little errors.
- You know what to do to find and fix capitalization, usage, punctuation, and spelling mistakes. Go for it.

Your corrections stand corrected! It's time for the unveiling…

Chapter 13

SHARE

Going Public with Your Essay

By the time my student Evelyn finished her essay, she was excited to show it to the world. She handed her essay to anyone who asked for it. They wanted to see it, so Evelyn thought, *Why not show it to them?*

I will tell you why not.

Evelyn leaped at the chance for a coveted appointment with the single college counselor for the 401 seniors at her public high school. (That's roughly the national average ratio of college counselors to students, so if you have more counselor access, you're lucky.) Her counselor had some suggestions about Evelyn's essay because it is her job to help students and provide feedback.

What the counselor said: "I'm not sure what you mean by *everything* in the second sentence. You could specify and tighten your intro a little bit."

What Evelyn heard: "You need a total rewrite."

Evelyn's mom, an attorney, took a red pen to Evelyn's essay, crossed out all Evelyn's lovely action verbs and appropriately conversational transitions, and replaced them with stuffy résumé words like *fostered* and *heretofore*. "You need to sell yourself more," said her mother, who clearly had not read this book.

What Evelyn heard: "You need a total rewrite."

Most of Evelyn's peer readers said they liked her essay, but one person in her AP Physics class (who Evelyn later admitted she didn't even know that well) thought the essay did not sound like her. Evelyn's best friend said, "I don't know about the word *plentiful* in a personal essay — it doesn't sound like something you'd say."

What Evelyn heard: "You need a total rewrite."

Everyone who read Evelyn's essay had an opinion, as people do. Some opinions were more informed than others, and after hearing from twenty-plus people, it was hard for Evelyn to discern the difference. Her Inner Troll burst free from its attic jail and wreaked havoc on her confidence. By the time I received Evelyn's call for help, her mind was like a Wild West saloon shoot-out.

At the other end of the spectrum, when Melanie had traveled as far as she could go it alone on her essay writing adventure and reached this point, her reaction was the opposite of Evelyn's. The thought of showing her essay to anyone at all petrified Melanie. It can be *terrifying* to open yourself up and share your labor of love with outside readers who might not understand.

Through the past couple of chapters, you and your Inner Editor were an unstoppable team, and you have a powerful essay before you. You have celebrated all this effort, which you deserve. (If not, stop reading and celebrate now.)

Still, we all need a little help. At the right time (now), outside input can prove extremely useful. You've finally reached the moment to hand over your essay to others for feedback. In this chapter, I will provide all the tools you'll need to increase the odds the feedback you receive is productive, rather than incapacitating, as it was for Evelyn. Or if you're anything like Melanie, it can be nerve-racking to share such a personal piece of writing, and not everyone is right for the job of reading it.

Choose Your Best Readers

You want readers who are invested enough in your success that they're willing to sacrifice their time to read your essay and respond quickly, but not *so* invested they attach their own baggage to their feedback. This is your call and *your* essay to show (or not show) to whomever you want.

Some options for readers with great potential

- ***A teacher*** can be an excellent resource. Choose the teacher who knows you best (not necessarily an English teacher), but please remember, teachers are not paid to provide feedback on your college essay (or to write college recommendations). They perform these unpaid tasks out of the kindness of their hearts, so requests during school vacations or at the last minute are not cool.
- ***A friend*** can make a good reader, but not just any friend. Resist sharing your essay with that competitive frenemy who is begging to read it.
- Great if you know ***a professional writer***, especially one with experience in personal essay or creative nonfiction writing (which is what you've been doing, in case you didn't realize).
- ***A trusted relative*** like an uncle or grandparent you respect could work, especially one who has a little critical distance from you so they can be honest. This brings us to the topic of parents, who are likely willing to sacrifice their time for you and certainly invested in your success.
- Using ***parents*** as readers is a personal choice (yours, not theirs). One of your parents might be a fantastic reader and (let's face it) the only person available if you waited until the last minute. (I'm not shaming you. Just sayin'.) Or your parent might be too emotionally invested in the outcome of your college admission odyssey to serve as a valuable reader for you.

Pick Two or Three Readers, Not Everyone You Know

You need the perspective of outside readers, but too many different opinions can overwhelm, leaving you vulnerable to fear and self-doubt. By oversharing, Evelyn invited her Inner Troll to behave badly and burgle her confidence. Let's avoid that mistake, okay?

Help Your Readers Help You

Not all feedback is created equal. Even readers with the best intentions can deliver discouraging criticism that will bring you down. To point readers in the right direction to provide worthwhile notes you can use, hand them a copy of the Reader's Guidelines on the next page. You can go on my website, JillShulman.com, and download these guidelines to make this easy. Then follow the Rule of Five Strategy and stay busy doing life while you wait for their feedback.

The Rule of Five Strategy

Brain Booster

Instructions

We all hope our readers will like our writing, but exclusively positive feedback is not the request. You're asking for honesty and constructive criticism, and you're gonna get it. The Rule of Five Strategy can help you keep the feedback you receive in perspective.

The Rule of Five: If it won't matter in five years, it is not worth five seconds stressing about it.

This rule is flexible. *Will the thing I'm anxious about matter in five weeks? five hours? five minutes?* It's shocking how often the answer is *no*. In five years, you'll likely graduate from college. Isn't that wild? By then, whatever your readers today say about your college application essay will be long forgotten.

Reader's Guidelines

Thank you so much for taking the time to help me with my personal essay for my college application. I'd appreciate any feedback you have in response to the following questions.

1. What do you think this essay is about? Can you summarize it in a sentence?
2. What will you remember most about my essay after reading it?
3. What might someone who doesn't know me learn about me from reading the essay?
4. Would you recognize that I was the one who wrote it? Does it sound like me?
5. Did you find any part of the essay confusing or unclear?
6. Is there anything that could be misread or concerning to a college that I may not have intended?
7. Do I come across as thoughtful and reflective?
8. Is there anywhere I could add more detail to make the essay clearer or more interesting, or conversely, is anything off-topic or extra that wouldn't be missed if it were cut?
9. Did you find any grammatical errors or awkward phrasing?
10. Are there any other small changes I could make to improve this essay?

How to Stay Confident in the Face of Feedback

Tips for Receiving Feedback Without Flipping Out

No one was suggesting Evelyn needed a total rewrite, and I doubt any of your readers are suggesting you need a total rewrite either. Harness useful feedback and discard the rest. Use these tips to preempt self-doubt when confronted with your readers' notes.

Say *Thank you, thank you, thank you.*

That was awfully generous of your readers to sacrifice their time and energy on your behalf, don't you think? The readers you chose are your allies (like me), and they are crucial to improving your writing. You are lucky to have them. No matter whether their feedback contained mostly praise or *many* suggestions, thank them (again).

Listen and take notes.

It's hard to remember everything said in the moment, especially if you have (*ahem*) feelings about the feedback you're hearing. You can refer to your written notes later, after you take a few deep breaths and use the Rule of Five Strategy to regain perspective. This one reader's feedback will not matter in five years. And it might benefit you in five minutes when you apply the helpful suggestions to your writing.

Don't interrupt to defend yourself or your essay.

Focus on listening, gathering information, and feeling gratitude for the fresh perspective. This is your reader's *opinion*, not an invitation for a debate. Sure, you asked for feedback, but that doesn't mean you have to use it. Black-and-white thinking, such as *They are wrong*, *They hate it*, or *They love it* is Inner Troll jibber jabber.

Your readers' suggestions do not mean you need a total rewrite or your essay is so perfect you can afford to tune out advice that could prove useful. Maintaining your positive, proactive mindset is a superpower you've mastered to crush this essay. Work it as you absorb important input.

Tips for Applying Constructive Feedback to Your Writing

Use only helpful advice.

Implement your readers' feedback that makes sense to you and politely ignore the rest. Not everything every reader suggests needs fixing. Trust your instincts. You have always held the power over your own essay, and you still do.

Think small improvements, not an overhaul.

When you first hear reader suggestions, they can sound like more work than they really are in practice. A friendly reminder: This is a moment for fine-tuning, not labor-intensive big-picture revisions. Listen for the opportunities your kind reader found to make your essay a wee bit better.

Look for common themes in your readers' comments.

Compare your notes from all your readers' feedback. Pay special attention when you notice that two or more readers made similar comments. Overlap indicates a higher chance that improvements in that part of your essay will strengthen it.

Correct mistakes readers catch.

Proofreading help for grammar and objective technical errors is always a bonus. Your readers may catch typos or other mistakes you missed. (More gratitude.) Fix the grammar and spelling mistakes your readers caught. Make any small changes you agree with to make your essay clearer, to correct mistakes, and to add a touch of pizzazz.

Remind yourself that *perfect* is the enemy of *finished*.

If you feel like you need one more reader (okay, two more), so be it. But please don't be a masochist and show your essay to ten more people. You heard what happened to Evelyn when she did so, and it wasn't pretty. Writing and revising can go on as long as you let them — potentially forever — but you have a whole life to enjoy beyond this one piece of your college application.

You have one final writing exercise to make tweaks based on advice you've received. You are so close to finishing your college essay. (Cue fireworks!)

The Last Pass

Writing Exercise

Instructions

1. **Incorporate into your essay all your readers' advice** that makes sense to you (and disregard the rest).
2. **Make final cuts,** if you're over the maximum word count permitted, to whittle the essay down to 650 words or fewer (or the word limit of the application you're using). Respect the service those cut words provided to your essay's creation as you bury them alongside their compatriots in the Expired Words Graveyard.
3. **Proofread your whole essay again.** Pay extra-close

attention to all the places where you just made changes. That's where most mistakes happen.

Dodge Common Essay Submission Snafus

Remember to delete readers' comments.

If your outside readers shared written thoughts with you in Google Docs or through Microsoft Word's Track Changes, make sure you *accept* (or *reject*) all changes and delete all comments before you upload your essay onto the application. You do not want Uncle Sylvester's margin comments visible to college admission evaluators.

Proofread yet again *after* uploading your essay onto the application.

One year, for no apparent reason, the Common Application cut off the last paragraph of some applicants' 650-word personal essays. One student told me she didn't realize her last paragraph was missing until after she'd submitted her application to twelve colleges. Eek. She had to contact all twelve admissions offices and hope they'd read the corrected essay version she emailed to them the next day. Another student reread the essay he'd already submitted early to a few colleges and saw a typo in a last-minute change he'd made to the first sentence. After all that work, it would anguish me if anything like that happened to you (and now it won't).

Fun Fact: You can change anything you want between submissions.

If you catch a typo after you've submitted your application to a college, it's there to stay (though one little typo won't destroy your chances for admission). But no need to let that typo linger for the next college to see. You can change anything you want on your application between submissions to different colleges.

No second-guessing.

You did a scary thing (exposing your heart and soul on the page for strangers to read) with confidence and poise. No overanalyzing what you could have, should have written. Once you've pressed the *submit* button, all I want you to feel is a flood of relief, pride, and joy because crafting your college essay from nothing to knockout was truly a rite of passage.

Set Up Your Reward System

Brain Booster

Look what you did! You completed your college essay—yeah, you did that. Celebrate this gigantic triumph and plan for the next. Milestones you achieve during your college *application* process are more important for your personal development than where you get into college. Truth.

Instructions

Choose among the rewards suggested in the Celebrate Interim Wins exercise in chapter 6, and celebrate when you:

- upload your personal essay onto the Common Application
- find and fix a run-on sentence or pump up a verb or two to improve a school paper for the first time
- use a Brain Booster technique from this book to keep perspective on a setback or disappointment

- hand your next essay (whether it's for a school assignment or for college admission) to a reader for feedback
- receive feedback on that essay without freaking out
- press the *return* key to submit your first college application
- press the *return* key to submit your last college application

While you're in celebration mode, don't let everyday victories pass you by without a nod. Acknowledge with a little treat each micro step you take to accomplish more than you had ten minutes ago.

This book ends with a gift for you, so read on to unwrap it.

Epilogue

Confidence Unleashed! Now for the Rest of the College Quest

Sonia, who began her college search interested in attending a big university, emailed me with the news that she had changed her mind. She had applied early and was admitted to her small liberal arts dream college. Evelyn told me she was admitted to her safety school (a college she had assumed would accept her) early action, but upon reflection, she's excited about it and might enroll there regardless of where else she gets in. Tyler thought he wanted to attend a small college where he could play ice hockey, and he had scouted the ones that also offered engineering programs. However, now Tyler is enthused about a college of liberal arts within a huge university. Go figure.

There is so much I want to say to you at the end of our journey together. Mostly, I want you to know that like Sonia, Evelyn, and Tyler, you will continue to grow and change minute by minute. If you stay open and flexible, notice what you're noticing, and break for appreciation moments, you'll find joy in the most extraordinary places — even if you land at an unexpected college studying a surprise major you never would've considered only months earlier.

Fun fact: About 80 percent of college undergraduates change their major before they graduate.

As you seize this moment to celebrate, I want to make sure

you know the reasons for celebration, which may be different than you would have guessed before you picked up this book.

Why What You Just Did Matters Moving Forward (Perhaps Not for the Reasons You Thought)

You believed you could, and you did.

Yes, you completed a knockout college essay (bravo!), but what you really did was empower yourself to take charge of your life. My dream is that you'll maintain that confidence throughout the rest of your college admissions adventure and beyond. Revel in the journey instead of fixating on results, and you will stay calmer and happier. Strike a power pose and imagine a cape flapping behind you.

You learned a lot about yourself.

All those soul-searching exercises you did to add depth to your essay can inform the rest of your college application process — and even your life choices, beginning with which college you select to attend. Please note that I said which college *you* select, not which college selects you.

Fun fact: It is not hard to get into college.

There are over four thousand colleges in the US alone, and well over half of those colleges admitted 50 percent or more of the students who applied in 2024. Up to 30 percent of colleges have *open admission* policies and accept everyone. No matter what your GPA, you have options and the power to choose among them. Summon your Inner Superhero to help you tune out the bombardment of voices from media, peers, and your Inner Troll telling you what you "should" do. You've learned to swap stress for excitement, and you can flip the script toward positivity, productivity, and empowerment at any time.

While on the college search, think, *Where do I want to go?* not *Which college will accept me?*

When choosing your future college, think, *What does success mean to me?* not *Which college will make me look successful to other people?*

When you arrive at college, keep asking yourself (as you have all along while writing your essay), *What do I want to say?* not *What do others want to hear?*

Continue to make life decisions from your heart and a place of confidence, and they will accumulate to form a path to your personal version of success (which you will modify with time and experience). Where you go to college is only the first big decision you'll make along the long, twisty, exciting road ahead.

You gathered writing tools and knowledge to improve your future writing.

I guarantee you'll need the critical writing skills from this book in countless impending scenarios, including college and on the job. (Yes, future engineer, you will still need to write memos and reports to your boss, who will feel vindicated that she made the right decision to hire you when she sees all those active verbs agreeing with one another.) Use AI when it serves you, but please remember that you are AI's master and not the other way around. You've proven yourself as an intelligent, capable writer all on your own. Bring this independent spirit and your Proofreading Shortcut Sheet with you to college and use them in good health.

You have completed a personal essay you can feel proud of.

You wrote four essay drafts and countless words along the way, managed to shear many of those words off your essay (may they rest in peace), made heaps of decisions, dug deep (and deeper), weathered feedback without crumbling, fiddled, polished, and completed your personal essay for your college application. Approach writing the rest of your application with the same boldness. Always write your first draft like no one will ever read it (they won't).

You conquered fear to reach a difficult goal.

Fear of the unknown is part of the human condition. I deeply hope one or more of the Brain Boosters in this book is a keeper for you. You can apply those anxiety busters to any stressful situation you face. (There will be plenty of them in your senior year alone.)

If your anxiety ever feels debilitating for any reason (or no reason at all), you are never alone. Asking for help when you recognize you need it is a sign of inner strength.

Emergency resources:

- ***Text 988 if you're in an immediate mental crisis.*** This number will connect you to the national Suicide & Crisis Lifeline for direct access to mental health professionals. *741741* is another number to text that will connect you with instant help from the nonprofit organization Substance Abuse and Mental Health Services Administration (SAMHSA).
- ***Talk to a parent, school counselor, or other trusted adult.*** Whether it's someone at home, school staff, or a coach or clergy member outside of school, please tell them you need help. They will support you and assist you to find it.
- ***Find a therapist by calling 1-800-662-HELP (4357).*** SAMHSA also runs this national helpline, which offers free, confidential treatment referrals and information 24-7.

You are a brave, strong, *confident* college applicant regardless of what happens next.

Your Inner Troll is jailed. You have tools to keep it incarcerated while you write the rest of your college application, nail your deadlines, and face other high-stakes situations. Let that Inner Troll of yours fester in prison for a life sentence. If it escapes and commits more crimes of confidence, your Inner Superhero now knows how to handle it. You are a rock star; play air guitar. (No one is watching.)

Now you can turn on your phone and post and text away. You've got this — all of it. Thank you for having faith and trusting me on this grand writing adventure. I have a world of faith in you too. It has been an honor to serve as your guide and ally against your Inner Troll's wicked whisperings. I'm excited for you and all your adventures ahead, and I am up here in the bleachers rooting for you.

You've earned a parting gift to tack onto your bedroom or future college dorm room wall…

Forward March Mantras

If you believe you can, you will.

Enthusiasm is contagious.

Get out of your own way.

Trying is the victory.

Becoming more comfortable with the uncomfortable is part of the adventure.

Inhale. Exhale. Repeat.

Ditch the idea of perfect.

What if it's not a problem?

Celebrate interim wins.

Invite awesomeness.

If it won't matter in five years, it is not worth five seconds stressing about it.

Embrace your power.

Appendix

A Baker's Dozen of Successful Student Essay Examples

The following are college application essays written by real former students of mine (with pseudonyms to protect anonymity), along with their genuine college majors. The essays appear here in the order the students are referenced in the book.

Caution: The essays included in this Appendix are not first drafts. The writers traveled through at least four drafts (Priya wrote nine!) before they uploaded the completed essay you'll read here onto a college application. Comparing your rough draft to a polished personal essay published in a book would be inviting your Inner Troll to heckle you, and we'll have none of that.

Most importantly, the essays in this Appendix are not yours. Use these essays as examples, as I've done when referring to them throughout this book, but not as templates to follow. Enjoy reading them for entertainment, inspiration, ideas, and motivation for self-discovery. Then close this book, look inward, and write the essay that is already inside you bursting to spill onto the page.

Tyler

Economics and European Studies double major

I'm standing where I always pictured myself standing in the granite hallway, behind the plain silver steel door. I have always been worried about tripping over the ledge right before we go on the ice, particularly before games. That's when everyone is watching. No one else seems to have an issue with it, even the other goalies on the team, but the ledge is just a little bit too tall, and I'm thinking that, standing in the tunnel, decked in my blue and gold jersey. That ledge is always in the back of my mind, just like the thought of a shoe coming untied during the championship track meet, or worrying about leaving a typo in an article I write for the school newspaper, or if that one tuft of hair that I couldn't comb down is still sticking up during a date. Little worries like this always seem to distract me, making it easier to focus on this small, surmountable problem before addressing the bigger, more urgent challenge ahead.

Our warm-up music starts to play. We have a few different playlists we use on game day, but I know which combination of electric music will bump over the speakers when I hear the first song. The music reverberates into our space behind that steel door, mixing with the yells and whoops of my teammates. I will never forget what I am about to do because I'll only get my first ice hockey start once. I remember publishing my first article in the newspaper, my first race that I ever ran, and the first girl I ever kissed. I'm hoping this will go a little bit better than all three of those firsts.

Coaches, teammates, trainers, the whole team lines up down the hallway behind the door, the starting goalie first, which today, is me. To be a goalie, one has to be a degree of crazy because what right-minded person would ever strap on pads and jump in front of a piece of vulcanized rubber flying at 90 mph for fun? The pressure used to make me sick before every hockey game I played as a kid but I felt so much better afterward that I could go into each game knowing that being sick was probably the worst thing that would happen to me all day, and now all I had to do was stop a puck.

I have an appetite for pressure, it seems. In track, I run the 800m and the 4x400m relay, both grueling, pressure cooker events. I still get nervous before races sometimes, particularly when I'm responsible for that last leg of the 4x400m. When I see my teammate hauling himself down that final straight, his arm stretched out with the baton in hand, the rest of the world goes silent, except for my own breathing and heartbeat. But when the baton lands in my hand, the screaming of my coaches and teammates comes rushing back. I can hear the footsteps of my competitors, but I never feel nervous then, because once I'm out on that track with the baton in my hand, there is no chance that I'm losing that race. I have to be the hero for my team in this last straightaway.

I've always wanted to be the guy that the little kids look at and drop their jaws in awe as he walks by. A few little kids wait beside the door to the ice, looking for that fist bump from the players as we walk by. After we pass, they'll all look at each other and grin and giggle with excitement. I push open the door and give those little guys a fist bump before I turn and take in the bright lights in front of me. The ice is empty, the stands are packed, and I didn't trip on the ledge that was just a little too tall.

Melanie

Psychology and Sociology double major

Truths About Living in Tiny Houses (and Grand Canyons)

It is a lifestyle choice.

My life goal (even if I don't pursue it until I'm eighty-five) is to build myself a functional, maximum-500-square-foot tiny house that I can haul across the nation to see all the national parks and experience every state, including Alaska. The adventurous tiny house lifestyle isn't for everyone, and honestly, I didn't think it was for me until I spent two weeks rafting down the Grand Canyon. The morning of our departure, twenty teenaged strangers stood on the shore of the Colorado River beside flimsy yellow rafts, feet sunk in the sand, not knowing what was expected of us. Like a broken record, the thought that this whole trip was a mistake played on a loop in my head. In front of us, bearded river guides hustled around the rafts securing paco pads, coolers, and water guns. One with an Indiana Jones hat walked toward us. "The river is brutal, but I already know one thing," he said. "You are all women warriors, and you are strong!"

If you want to survive in a tiny house, you must get rid of a lot of your junk.

Anxiety can be a heavy bag to bear, and I've carried more than my fair share of it. As a child, whenever my dad left on business trips, I'd become anxious about robbers or monsters sneaking into my room, so I slept with my mom. So my dad created an abysmal artist's rendition of a medieval-looking shield inscribed with a D for Davis. He taped it to my bedroom door forcing anxious thoughts (plus the robbers and monsters) to dissipate before they could enter. Flying to the Grand Canyon triggered an anxiety attack. My mind wouldn't shut up: plane falling out of the sky, all the girls on the trip hating me, dying in the middle of the desert, and my family moving forward without me. The irrational fears were all-encompassing.

It isn't easy.

Twenty women ranging from extremely athletic to the athletically challenged walked upstream between tall rock walls until we came to an impasse. The only way out was to go up. While each woman struggled to climb up the slippery rock, we clapped and cheered. When my turn came, I became more and more anxious as I ascended, but in a different, more rational way. In my head, my father, holding his shield, climbed beside me, and along with the support of the women around me, even when my foot slipped, I recovered easily and kept moving upward with a newfound confidence. At the summit, we yelled, "We are women warriors! We are strong!"

It promotes bonding.

If you asked my mom, she would tell you I have an amazing voice, but do consider the source. Our cozy little glob of people sat on the rock floor of a massive cave singing "Electric Love." Some of us were talented singers, others monotoned, and others silent swayers. We identified as Cuban, Arab, African, Greek, bisexual, homosexual, heterosexual, Christian, Mormon, Jewish, and atheist. A stream of sunshine entered through the mouth of the cave and warmed the burnt orange of its river-carved walls. I swayed and sang at the top of my lungs alongside twenty women and five outdoorsmen I had only recently met. Like a family is connected by blood, we were bound together by the desert magic.

There is always space for the most meaningful things in a tiny house.

My old irrational anxieties will not fit into my future tiny house. It will be filled with my dad's shoddy family shield and my cozy glob of friends singing "Electric Love," slightly off-key, echoing from room to room, across the nation, to college, and beyond. In the Grand Canyon, I started building its foundation.

Billy

Computer Science major

If reward > risk:
They were serving putrid-smelling burritos in the cafeteria the day I met Nate and Scott for the first time. My mom had made me a salami sandwich with mustard, which was not my favorite, although I said nothing because complaining would only result in the true statement that I should make my own lunch. Plus, it was better than the burritos. Nate and Scott seemed intent and focused on this card game, Magic: The Gathering (MTG), with the sort of concentration I admired. When I approached them, I was 60% interested in the game, 40% thinking these people seem nice. After a subpar first half of the year at my new school, socially speaking, I hoped to finally make some cool friends (cool from my relatively nerdy perspective). I asked if I could join.

If MTG == Played:
    Life = "changed"
Over the time of one MTG match, I can go from knowing nothing about a person to knowing a lot about their personality. Nate is a controlling MTG player. He plays cards that slow the game down to his pace. In life, he likes to be the leader. When we play Dungeons and Dragons, we play at Nate's house, and he's the dungeon master. Scott is really good with numbers. He calculates which path will win and which path will cause the most damage before playing his cards. I like problem-solving, too, but I prefer decks that are dynamic and fun to play. Usually my decks don't win, but I enjoy when the synergies between cards are cool, uncommon, and sometimes powerful. I'm not about playing for control or stopping people from doing their thing. I'm about doing my own thing and savoring the crazy interactions that unfold.
Def change(person):

I almost always have something new to obsess over, and MTG is my latest. In middle school, my obsessions would center around a book series like *Harry Potter* or *Divergent* or video games I played alone. However, playing MTG enabled me to channel my inner nerd into a social experience in high school. I still have my obsessions, but now I share and discuss them with friends, and they introduce me to new obsessions like the web comic Homestuck. I consider this my reward for having the guts to introduce myself to Nate and Scott that day at lunch.

If Cards == Coding:
Magic: The Gathering is like writing a piece of code, which I also love to do. In MTG, you fit each creature into its slot to block others' plays and try to win. In coding, every argument, variable, function, and class is its own piece of a big puzzle with infinite ways to finish it. In python, specifically, there's a function called *time.sleep*, which causes the program to pause for a few seconds. MTG is my *time.sleep* command. It helps me escape from the next test, the next chore, the next whatever. For half an hour or so, nothing else matters beyond how to fit the pieces I have into the current puzzle configuration before we have to get back to class.

Return (win)
In one recent game, I lost and won at the same time. Lunch was half over, and I hadn't even started eating yet. Nate had slowed the game down to a crawl with his winter orb. Scott did some simple math, untapped his mana, and swung all his creatures at me, betraying our previous alliance. I was ejected from the game through Scott's treachery! I put away my cards and unpacked my (self-made) turkey and cheese sandwich. Playing more defensively would have been a safer move, but taking the risk was definitely worth it. Either way, I knew I'd win. I would win the game, or I'd get to eat my lunch with my best friends. Both outcomes seemed like victories to me.
Return person, change

Karina

Astrophysics major

The dress caught my eye first. Multiple layers of blue, purple, and white floaty fabric flared and drifted softly behind her as the current world figure skating champion, Evgenia Medvedeva, spun and jumped. A galaxy of white gems clustered in a starburst right above her skirt. Every step and swirl glittered. Figure skating had always been an Olympic favorite of mine, but when I saw Evgenia skate in PyeongChang, it was almost like watching it for the very first time. Evgenia's gentle movements seemed weighed down with sadness. I felt certain I understood the story she told of mourning something she had lost but coming to terms with it.

I've always been drawn to stories, especially fantasy. I read *Harry Potter* when I was seven, the *Percy Jackson* series in second grade, and in the back corner of my third-grade classroom, I delved deeper into mythology. A gap between the shelves created a little hiding space, where I would retreat into the pull of the stories.

Then on a sixth-grade field trip to Camp Grady Spruce, one night we spread blankets on a field so we could lie down and look up. One of the counselors, Andy, took out a laser pointer and started sketching out star constellations in the sky. It was a warm night, the smell of bug spray thick in the air as Andy spoke. There was an uptick in noise when he pointed out Orion, several students breaking out in the song about Orion we'd been singing in music class since first grade. I was one of them. After we quieted down, Andy turned our attention toward Cygnus, the swan. I was long past my Greek Mythology phase but I remembered Cygnus. I liked that there was a swan made of stars, a simple cross shape but I imagined the curling feathers and outstretched wings of a swan superimposed over it. Even after Andy moved on, I tried to picture the swan flying across the night sky and remembered the stories I had read.

The myths are full of young men who become swans, often after dying, and many end in immortalizing a character in the sky, either to honor or punish them. My introduction to astronomy made me wonder if the myths changed when constellations were established, or if constellations were established to strengthen the truth of the myth. Anything can happen in stories you make up but in science, laws and theories govern how things work. I was drawn to astronomy because ultimately, the stars are just balls of compressed gas, bound to move forever in their prescribed orbits. But when people look up into the sky, they don't see helium and hydrogen; they see stories.

Like astronomy, skating combines the science and stories I love. The movements themselves are governed by the laws of physics and the rule book, but you can combine them in any way you want to write your own story on the ice. Inspired by Evgenia's 2018 Olympic performance, I began skating myself. My coach speaks equally about the physics of certain moves and the importance of making it all look graceful and effortless. Unlike Evgenia, I'm no prodigy — I still struggle with some of the basic steps — but I'm definitely improving.

My back outside edges are still somewhat unsteady, but the strong, sweeping motions of my skates' inside edges make me feel powerful as I curve my way along the perimeter of the rink to gather speed. Mohawk into back crossovers, twist my upper body, step out, lean, kick up, fold my arms to reduce air resistance, and then — I'm in the air. It's just half a rotation, but I cover a good meter and a half of ice, and it's enough to feel like I'm flying. Sometimes I feel like if I jump high enough, I'll become a constellation in the stars.

Cassidy

Visual Studies major

Reds, whites, pinks, browns, and blues swirl, vibrate, then form circles and lines, horizon and sky. The shapes morph into a group of children, all dressed identically in red and white school uniforms. Their scarlet sweaters and wide smiles contrast sharply with the muted background of a weathered blue, single-story school building with an aging tin roof. As the camera zooms in, I finally spot Mika among the sea of students. She clutches a worn book, with her hair fashioned in uniquely patterned braids.

Pale peach. Light yellow. Periwinkle blue. Even though I know there is a whole world outside of this painting, all I can focus on in this moment is that Mika's skin is not vibrant enough, and it just needs more burnt sienna.

The art studio lights are turned off, so only natural light is streaming in through the floor-to-ceiling wall of windows. Perched on my favorite paint-splattered metal stool, I contemplate. How do I get Mika's smile just right? I hope she likes lilac for the background color.

My internal questions take hours and days to answer. Through the painstaking process of creating Memory Project portraits, I become connected to each child. Studying Mika's face for over twenty hours, I feel this powerful and personal attachment to her. The jagged scar on her forehead, her crooked bottom teeth, her circular hot-pink earrings, are each integral parts of this child. As the artist, it is my job to combine these seemingly disparate pieces to make an authentic, whole image. I desperately yearn to capture not just what Mika looks like, but who she is.

Golden yellow. Sunset orange. Royal blue. The camera zooms in until Mika's familiar face appears, side by side with my portrait of her. Seeing my painting come to life is surprisingly emotional. I proudly notice that I successfully captured the way her upper lip crooks up more on the left side. And look! She is wearing the pink earrings! Mika's onyx eyes exude warmth and stare directly into the camera as she says in accented English, "My name is Mika. Thank you for the beautiful painting. I love it very much. Thank you, Cassidy."

Mika's image lingers with me long after the video ends. Her undeniable and universal humanity moves me. While painting Mika, I have realized that she is so much more than an orphan 7,650 miles away in Nairobi, Kenya. She is a beautiful and bright ten-year-old girl who rides bicycles, enjoys math, and adores *Harry Potter*, not unlike my own younger sister.

Coral. Magenta. Fuchsia. Connecting with others through art drives me to continue painting, not only for the Memory Project, but also for myself. I hope to travel to Kenya next summer to personally deliver Memory Project portraits to children at The Red Rose School. However, even if I finally meet Mika in person, I don't think I will feel any closer to her than I do now.

Sea-foam green. Lemon yellow. Turquoise blue. Color is how I connect with and see the world. My beloved puppy is lively greens, yellows, and oranges, while my grandparents' house in Sanibel feels like cheery pinks and blues. Conversely, my four concussions from basketball were achingly bleak, flat, almost colorless periods. The cumulative totality of my experiences makes my world increasingly vibrant and layered. In turn, the colors in my art become more complex, rich, and deep.

Pale peach. Light yellow. Periwinkle blue. There is no place in the world I feel more content and like myself than in the art studio. This crowded room of happy chaos, infused with the smell of turpentine and the soft hum of music through my headphones, is where I begin my next Memory Project painting. As Dillon's face emerges from my scattered brushstrokes, I again begin deliberating highlights and background colors. I cannot wait to see how painting this child will color my world.

Priya

International Studies major

"Nuke war causes nuke winter — cc and biod loss" (Nuclear war causes nuclear winter — leads to climate change and biodiversity loss).

I walk down the egg yolk colored hallway.

"Arms k2 working voters — swings 2020" (Arms sales are key to working-class voters — swings the election).

I climb down the stairs.

The smell of Pringles drifts from their backpacks as the novices breathe heavily into their computers trying to catch their breath between strings of disjointed words. These are the hallways of my high school an hour before we pile into a school bus for the annual Lexington Debate Tournament.

The incoherent phrases remind me of my second week on the debate team as a freshman when I had just started to learn spreading (the combination of the words "speed" and "reading"), the common language of the debate world. By cramming more arguments into a speech, it makes responding harder and winning easier. Two hundred words per minute: terrible. 300 wpm: average. 400 wpm: threatening.

While doing spreading drills with my teammates at school, I quietly read into my book so that no one could hear how slow I was. Then, at home, I picked the longest article I could find and timed myself as I spread through it for eight minutes. I read it again with a pencil in my mouth. I read it backwards. I read it so that each word had the word "watermelon" or "Oreo" after it, all drills to make me faster. Then I tried again. I only spread at 150 wpm: disgraceful.

Though I wasn't speedy at first, the debate community welcomed me and taught me their traditions. For instance, at the Harvard Debate Tournament, our opponents and my teammates stood across from each other as if they were about to duel. To an outsider, this was a mere coin flip to pick sides (affirmative or negative), but to me, the coin spun in slow motion as we watched. Whoever won the flip controlled the round! As a little girl and an only child, my colorful plastic Playmobile companions truly shared all of my values. As I grew older, my friends shared some of them. But once I joined my new debate world, I was surrounded by real people who understood completely why something as minuscule as a coin flip mattered so much. Just like coin flips, I learned that "debate clout" (for me, intimidating my opponents with punk rap music) and fancy timers (phone timers are for amateurs) are all part of debate's secret society of unwritten rules.

As I became a more experienced debater, I gained confidence to take more risks. In every aspect of my life, I began channeling my debate confidence into engagement. In class, I projected my voice and initiated discussions, the same way I did at debate tournaments, instead of speaking only to join conversations. I explored philosophies that I never knew existed and learned about international relations, politics, and the government for debate competitions, which inspired my prospective career path in law. At home, debate became my ticket into my parents' dinner table conversations. Although I was never the "most valuable eater" (MVE), my input in family conversations grew as I became more well versed in current events.

"DP will be replaced with LWOP" (The death penalty will be replaced with life-without-parole).

The debaters spread their last words before the bus leaves for Lexington. They have stumbled into a community of people who care about the same things I do and, as their debate team Captain, I'm guiding them along the same journey I took. Learn the language, gain the confidence, and apply it. What started as a weird fast-talking challenge transformed the way I act, think, and perceive the world around me. And I have graduated from a phone timer to a professional debate timer. My latest spreading is 378 wpm: on the verge of formidable.

Levi

Computer Science major with Philosophy minor

Snow tracking is hard. The prints aren't completely clear, but I can still make out the little X of negative space formed between foot pads. The "canine X," we call it. But which canine? All is revealed — as it so often is in wildlife tracking — with a yellow splotch on a mound of snow. I place my feet on one side of the trail and hands on the other to form a bridge over the tracks. With this pro strat I won't damage the trail, I'll get a core workout, and I'll get to smell the pee. That's three wins. I put my nose close to the stain (but not too close) and inhale deeply, then pause for a moment and look off contemplatively into the hemlock forest like a wine taster processing a fine vintage. There it is. The unmistakable skunky odor of red fox urine.

As excited as we trackers get by urine, it's nothing compared to scat. In the online tracking community that I run, most of the posts ask, "Whose poop is this?" When I first started tracking as a young camper at Earthwork Programs, I fell in love with the puzzles it presented (even when they didn't include excrement). I've always loved puzzles, from trying to figure out a tricky move at a rock-climbing competition with some of my teammates, to searching for the syntax error in my python program. But solving tracking mysteries feels special. It brings the outdoors to life. A hole in a tree becomes the sign of a pileated woodpecker searching for carpenter ants. A line of dents in the snow becomes the path of a waddling porcupine. "Tracking is, at its core, a practice in empathy and imagination," a mentor once told me, and now working as a counselor at Earthwork Programs, I share this with the campers. Following an animal's trail feels like decoding the story of its life.

To follow this fox trail, I have to duck through thickets of hemlock, clamber over stone walls and slide along a frozen stream of dubious structural integrity. Hunting for voles, the fox patters around a spot, ears perked up (I've seen videos of this), and then pounces, leaving a dent in the snow and drops of blood. Then the fox splits into two foxes (it's mating season!) weaving between trees, one moment walking in each other's footprints to conserve energy, and the next splitting apart, as if to prove their individuality.

The forest's canopy opens to bright sky as I follow the foxes into a channel of land cleared for power lines that functions as a wildlife highway. Every pad and dewclaw from moose to field mice is recorded precisely here in the warmer snow. The foxes' path takes me around boulders and power line poles mauled by black bears and up and down rolling hills patterned with trails of deer, hares, coyotes, and now, one curious human. Eventually, I lose the foxes' trail under the tracks of a herd of browsing deer in a thicket of brambles. I only get a tiny snapshot of their lives, but I imagine them still roaming that forest, eating and peeing (not so different from me).

Though I was lured by the puzzles, wildlife tracking has also become a ritual for me. It's refreshing to step away from my computer and the clamor of the rock-climbing gym to spend some time alone in the woods. It's calming to join the rhythm of nature in winter: silent and serene, interrupted only by the occasional startled grouse or snow shifting off a sagging hemlock branch leaving behind it a trail of glimmering white powder suspended in sunlight. This was the human experience for thousands of years before TV and social media. We were part of that rhythm. It's grounding returning to it. It's my reboot.

Lia

Biology major with Plant Biology concentration

Draw a circle in the sand to narrow the plane.

Hunt for a tiny black 'T' shape.

Knife-like serrations are a sure sign you've found one.

Once my grandma trained me to spot sharks' teeth, I couldn't stop seeing them. Staring at the sand's beige grains and quartz crystals, squatting beneath the blazing sun, inhaling the sulfuric odor of pluff mud, I could see why most people, like my dad and brother, hated this hobby. It required patience and a lot of time hunched over in the heat before finding anything. The marsh grass crackled in the wind. The waves slapped arrhythmically onto the shore. The soggy sand pulled at my shoes, but I kept searching.

I was introduced to a different kind of exploration through beekeeping. When I was seven, my Grandpa announced that he was going to help us set up an apiary. ("Look it up in the dictionary. No, I won't tell you how to spell it!") It requires courage or stupidity to don a bee suit, open a hive, and not run away when several thousand angry bees pour out. It took seven years and restarting from scratch three times before our hives were strong and successful. After years of waiting, we had to harvest the honey by slicing off the honeycomb, whirling frames in the extracting machine, then pouring and labeling the bottles. The harvesting process wasn't fun. I invariably got honey stuck in my hair and some irate bees usually snuck into the house, but participating in every step it took to fill those plastic bears made it the best honey I'd ever tasted.

I've never shied away from a tough endeavor, but I didn't expect my first mosaic to take so long to finish. I couldn't cut the glass pieces, and frustration set in as I realized that none of my red pieces would fit into an ugly gap in a swath of red on my tabletop rendering of two seahorses underwater. Shoving around the glass, my fingers grazing over pointy corners, I evaluated the blobs of color by analyzing their size and edges. I happened upon an arched black sliver of glass, crossed by two thin lines of orange and royal blue, that nestled into the open space above my mosaicked seahorse's eye. The perfect fit! (Every good seahorse needs eyebrows!) The piece stood out starkly from its surroundings, making my mosaic something entirely unique. This ended up taking the past three summers to complete, but I knew that even if I encountered another mosaic seahorse with an eyebrow, it could never be identical because of that colorful little arch of glass.

At the end of the day, a bottle of honey is a bottle of honey, a mosaic is a mosaic, and a shark's tooth is just a tooth. I could buy any of them, but I would never skim around the best parts of an experience just to rush to the end result. When I observe an object or process that piques my interest — bee behaviors or a composition of glass — I experiment and modify my hypotheses. Science as it appears in nature is ever-changing and always presents me with something exciting to find when I'm patient and take the time to look.

A sleek black surface glints in the sun.

Focus in on the slight curve of its edges.

Dust off the sand to make sure it's not a buried rock.

My vision narrowed and my breath caught. It was two inches long, a little crooked to the left, with itty-bitty serrations and the very tip cracked off. That probably doesn't sound impressive — definitely no megalodon — but there it was: the biggest shark's tooth I'd ever found. The sun scorched my back and my knees ached from squatting, yet still I flushed with excitement. I'd waited so long to find this tooth that was waiting for me.

Sonia

Environmental Studies major

Kyudo Step One, Yo-i, Obtain the Right Spirit

Myself, the bow, and the arrow stand in three parallel lines. My feet root into the ground. An imaginary thread stretches my spine upward. My arms lift round like a ballerina to hold a beach ball of energy. Slow, natural breaths calm my racing thoughts about school and the chaotic city beyond the studio's open windows.

My school garden is another escape. During a free period, a gardening club co-leader and I head to the raised beds for some seeding. I plunge my finger into the soil, then sprinkle three paper-thin milkweed seeds inside the burrow. I cover the seeds with cozy, dark compost. I repeat the process until the packet runs out. Finally, I drown the soil to soften the seeds. I will return as often as possible to tend the garden and relieve stress. My friend reminds me class starts in five minutes. Before I go, I crouch to examine the broad green leaf on an unexpected composted-cantaloupe seedling emerging.

Uchi Okoshi, Raise for Shooting

I connect the arrow tip to the target with my gaze. The ball of energy in my arms becomes weightless. My bow rises like mist. My back strains, pulling the bow to mouth level, but my mind keeps steady. My left hand becomes a tiger's mouth, "the way cats hold their babies, gently with the back of their jaws so as to not pierce them," Sensei says. I accept the damage I will deal to the target without pride or shame.

At home, the leggy, yellowing *Monstera deliciosa* in my parents' bedroom looks in dire need of help. I feel bad cutting what the plant worked hard to grow, so I snip one leaf at a time. But I know we need to let go of unhealthy parts to develop wholly. My cuts get more ruthless. When the job is done, the *Monstera*, though not as big, has a better chance of thriving.

Hanare, Release

The bow is drawn. Both eyes are open; my right aims. When my upper body twists to the left, Sensei says, "Don't get corrupted by the target." The tension between my inner meditation and outer strain builds like pressure in a balloon, eventually bursting into release. I rarely remember the moment of letting go. The string slings past my face, but I stay still. This moment of meditation matters more than seeing the arrow in the target.

The results aren't the most important part of gardening, either. That's why I've laid compost over my raised bed at home to prepare for some good ol' "chaos gardening." My mug of miscellaneous seeds overflows with sweet peas from Ocean State Job Lot, bird seed, chai masala, and old beans from the shed. I disperse, rake, and douse them. The seeds might be expired, or birds might eat them. They might grow. I'm more carefree about these things because the whole point of gardening to me is to escape worry over whether plans will work out. Everything I sow ends up back in the ground one way or another.

Zanshin, Linger in the Mind and Body

My mind is blank, my body open. I am at peace as my eyes meet the arrow's placement. I didn't hit the bullseye this time. With repetition, my blocky kyudo movements will begin to flow together like a dance.

Since its makeover, the sheared *Monstera* has flourished. In my chaotic raised beds, some seedlings decompose underground, while others reach for the light. It will take time to see if the milkweed in the school garden develops balls of orange flowers where monarchs can poke their curly proboscises. It's all part of the larger routine of watering, waiting, and watching. In archery and gardening all I have to do to hit my target is aim at hidden, beautiful moments of quiet observation. I have those to myself.

Max

Criminal Justice major, Pre-Law track

Structured, organized, disciplined; these are not qualities one would generally use to describe a toddler. However, that is what the first four years of my life were like in Orphanage 21, Moscow, Russia. Ten groups, ten kids in each, two caretakers per group, ten blue potty seats, ten tiny toothbrushes, ten toddler-sized beds. Awake time, meal time, bathroom time, play time, sleep time. Everything precise. It was the only way a Soviet-style, state-run orphanage, with almost no resources, worked. At four years old, I was the oldest in my group of ten. I had "responsibilities" to be helpful with the younger ones. Helpful leadership was instilled in me from the very beginning. In many ways, I am still that little boy.

The day I left the orphanage with my parents and sister began an era of "first times" for everything. It was my first time riding in a car, in an elevator, on an escalator, in an airplane, and landing in New York City. Wow! From a life with almost nothing to stimulate me, I entered a life with stimuli from every direction. It was the beginning of an incredible adventure, as my pre-adoption life rapidly faded into memories. I found myself living in a large, fancy, yellow, Colonial house in a typical American suburb twenty or so miles south of Boston. I had never been in such a big, colorful house before, with so many hallways and rooms that it felt like a maze. I was used to living in a building with uniform eggshell-white walls and beds lined up in rows of five. It felt strange sleeping alone; I couldn't look to my right and see my best friend, Ruseron. Instead, I looked to my right to find my very own white alarm clock sitting on my wooden nightstand in my new personal room.

As I got used to this new lifestyle, I started participating in town activities like soccer and horseback riding. I think because of my early childhood role as eldest at the orphanage, I found myself always wanting to help and lead the other kids around me. Back in Russia, Ruseron, a year younger, always followed me around. I was like a big brother to him. In elementary school, when I was team captain for playground games, I would act like a big brother to the kids who were not usually picked first to be on a team, and pick them first.

Although I loved it all, when I was introduced to Civil Air Patrol at fourteen, it was the first activity that resonated deeply with me. At my first Civil Air Patrol meeting, I was a little intimidated, seeing teenagers in military uniforms calling each other "Ma'am" and "Sir." But as I learned about all of the leadership training and discipline incorporation, I soon came to realize that this type of lifestyle was similar to the one I'd lived back in Russia, familiar and comfortable. Everything these cadets did in Civil Air Patrol — from wearing the uniform, to drills and ceremonies — made me feel like I had entered a new home with another family I wanted to be a part of.

My personality hasn't really changed during my transition from a Russian toddler in Orphanage 21, to an occasional team captain on an American elementary school playground, to a seventeen-year-old Cadet Commander leading and protecting my squad of cadets. Structured, organized, disciplined; these are not qualities one would generally use to describe a teenager, but all along, they've described me.

Stevie

Film and Media Studies major with Drama minor

The first "hat" I knitted was a twisted mess, too large for any head, far from something wearable. It was riddled with so many holes from dropped stitches that it wouldn't keep anyone warm. Yet, when I first walked into the dining hall at the Outdoor Academy (OA), bonnet proudly resting on my head, I was met with cheers from all twenty-seven other students. I most definitely looked funny wearing the enormous hat, but with months of work, patience, and the support of my community, I'd made something. That hat was *mine*.

Knitting was one of the many things that made the OA community unlike any other. At OA, everyone took care of each other, whether Jeremy helped me untangle a complicated math problem, or Adriana motivated Alex, the slowest among us, as we climbed a painfully steep mountain. We addressed real-world problems and asked the uncomfortable, difficult questions that are typically discouraged. Why do some people have so much while others have so little? Can empathy be learned? We functioned symbiotically, every individual giving and taking. At OA, I discovered what a community truly can be.

When I returned home to Atlanta, I struggled to transition from such a healthy, connected community of twenty-eight students to such a polarized one of seven million. Along with a few messy hats and a strong body from miles of backpacking, I brought home a new understanding of what it means to be part of a community: connection. Imagined boundaries of race, gender, class, and religion separated my city, and people treated each other terribly on these bases. School-aged children discarded restaurant leftovers only a few feet away from men begging for food, and women in Chanel coats walked past women shivering in rags. When I returned from OA, I witnessed the divisions in my city with new eyes and wondered what I, as an individual, could do to bridge them. I realized that knitting was a huge part of what brought my OA community so close together. And then it hit me — what if I could use that same skill to string together a larger community, even one of seven million?

In response, I founded Knitting Together Atlanta (KTA), a Georgia-based nonprofit organization, through which volunteers visit Atlanta homeless shelters and knit with the residents. KTA provides a skill, a sense of pride, and, most importantly, interactions that would otherwise not exist. I wanted to encourage conversations between the women in Chanel coats and the women with no coats. I registered my nonprofit, emailed shelters, and used social media to reach out to Facebook and Instagram knitting communities. Before I knew it, yarn donations from across the country piled into a soft, colorful heap taking up half my room, and people were coming to KTA events from all over Georgia to knit with people they'd never met.

Sitting at a large table covered with yarn balls and needles, the conversations came easily. The once group of strangers knitting together quickly became friends as we shared patterns for hats and scarves. When Mary, a shelter resident who had struggled with knitting for weeks, finally mastered the process, the room erupted into cheers as she began filling her circular needles with stitches. At the next KTA event, she'd nearly finished her hat! I explained how to decrease stitches, as my OA peers had done for me: knit two together, until you have no more to knit. That's how I hope to decrease divisiveness in my community of seven million people, one ball of yarn at a time. The smile on Mary's face lit up the room as she ceremoniously placed the hat on her head. Like my first hat, hers didn't fit right, and the pattern looked a little lopsided, but it was a beautiful hat, we all agreed.

Emilio

Biology major, Pre-Med track

My mom entered her office where I waited on the squishy red couch to start my shift and said, "Ready to lift that big boy?"

The bright pink pig lying in the lobby by the receptionist's desk weighed at least 100 pounds and had wrinkles and puffy circles beneath her eyes. Her breath was the sound of fatigue, like she'd just finished running a mile. I learned that the owners kept the pig inside and treated her like she was their own little puppy. She lay in a giant bed with tons of toys before her yearly check-up that required putting her under anesthesia.

Technicians in gray scrubs and my mom (the veterinarian) stood behind me, waiting. I thought to myself, *How am I supposed to lift that huge animal?* Sometimes I need motivation to pull myself out of my comfort zone. I thought, *I can do this. Nobody else can. I've got to step up*. Around the clinic, moving stuff and fixing things is what I'm there for. I've laid flooring, replaced cabinets, changed out the faucet — that was fun to figure out — and installed an electric table that could hold five people, which was where I needed to carry this pig.

The animal screamed louder the closer I got. Her eyes went from resting to wide open. I bent down in a squat and positioned my arms under her like I would lifting weights for baseball practice. Her rough hair dug into my arms. The pig screamed and scurried to the other side of the room as fast as she could, which was still pretty slow. When I tried again, I locked my hands as tightly as I could and carefully lifted her.

All the workers' eyes widened, mouths opened, and, like the pig, they squealed as I held her right up against my body, my head hovering above the pig's squirming torso, and began my cautious walk to the surgery table. The workers snapped to, running ahead to open all the doors. I walked seemingly forever (really about forty steps) through the lobby, down the hallway, and to the surgery room, where I stood hugging the 100-pound pig tight. Everything seemed in slow motion as workers threw blankets and towels on the table, prepped the anesthesia machine and oxygen tanks, and set up the surgical instruments. I used extreme focus, like I would on a calculus test or watching the baseball strike my bat, to steady the pig who continued to scream and squirm as I lowered her onto the table where a couple of workers and I held her down until the anesthesia knocked her out.

Then everyone yelled, "Yay Emilio, woo-hoo!"

My mom yelled loudest of all, smiling her thousand-megawatt smile, and I felt the same way I feel working at rabies clinics with her early on a Saturday morning each year, giving free rabies shots to animals whose owners can't afford them. I always want to be a part of the solution. I enjoy being the person who does the "heavy lifting." Completing a helpful job, even if it's just carrying a pig, gives me great satisfaction. Seeing my mom help animals, and her orthopedic surgeon friend I shadowed last summer help people, inspired me to pursue medicine in a specialty that I love and make an impact.

I was finishing some schoolwork while my mom examined the pig, when I heard, "Emilio!" and I hopped to it.

My mom, in all of her surgery PPE — gloves, gown, mask, and hair cover — stood over the knocked-out pig on the table. "Ready for one last lift, muscle man?" she said.

I love working at the clinic and being of service, but after I'd replaced the pig onto her bed in the lobby, I still hoped my mom's next patient would be a chihuahua.

Evelyn

Mathematics major

It sounds crazy, a drought in Vermont, but the lonesome steady stream I had used the day before to gather my water had disappeared. Deep in the rock's crevice, I noticed a drip: one drop per second with a one-centimeter diameter. I secured a handkerchief as a filter over my gallon bottle's top and placed it under the natural spout, mounted my favorite sitting rock, and began the wait.

Drip. Drip. Drip.

The only clock I had was the sun moving, east to west, toward trees I could use as tally marks.

tree1tree 2oz in bottle = x

32 ozx=# tree sun will reach when bottle full

According to my calculations, my water bottle would be full when the sun hit the fourth tree, about two hours.

Drip. Drip. Drip.

A chipmunk bolted toward me, my only company for the duration of my four-day solo wilderness experience at the Mountain School. The agreement with the wildlife was "I won't disturb you and you won't disturb me." Social contracts like these look slightly different outside the Vermont woods.

For example, in the driver's seat for the first time, when it was my turn at a four-way stop sign, a car rolled into the intersection. I screeched the brake, my heart racing, acutely aware of possible disaster every second on the road, where random humans blindly trust me with their lives, and I trust them with mine. In following road rules, I agreed to a life-or-death social contract, but how many less critical agreements did I submit to passively every day? My English teacher once described grammar as a means to convey clearly what I wanted to say so people could understand me, and politeness was an agent to build relationships of trust and respect, which made good sense to me. But what about the social expectations that exclusively applied to one group? I joined my computer science class freshman year as one of twelve girls; three years later, I was the sole girl remaining. I felt pressure to prove myself as a representative of all women, even though I had never struggled with coding any more than the boys. When I started Code At Home last summer, I aimed to teach computer skills to young girls, so that maybe one day, these girls could be role models and revise that antiquated social construct.

Drip. Drip. Drip.

The chipmunk's shadow dashed across my field of vision, leaves shuddering in its wake. The sun intersected the fourth tree, indicating my water bottle should have been full, but the last quarter of the bottle remained empty. The drops' rate had slowed. An unexpected variable my equation had not accounted for: "change."

One of my favorite parts of my solo wilderness experience was the way this strip of land felt like home after four days alone there, but in a few short months, it would all change. In autumn, fallen leaves would cover the bare soil lining the dried riverbed. By winter, the chipmunks would hibernate under snow, and I would not be settled on this rock waiting for my water bottle to fill. I would be back in New York City, where water is plentiful and the social contracts aren't as simple as "we will leave each other alone." But I'd return changed, with the new perspective that I had agency to sign onto only those social contracts that mattered to me and serve as a force for change for those that promoted inequity. Politeness, proper grammar, teaching younger girls to code, and stepping up to chair the Women's Leadership and Special Olympics clubs at my school were a start.

Drip. Drip. Drip.

Approximately two hours had passed, and the sun glowed equidistantly between the dried riverbed's banks, indicating it was nearly noon on the dot. My water bottle remained a quarter empty, but I could now see that it was also three-quarters full.

Acknowledgments

Something magical happened when I started writing this book and revisiting former students who had made an impact on me. As I recounted their stories, trials, successes, and the giddy joy of their *aha* moments, I relived the thrill of watching these remarkable young adults claim ownership of the next stage of their lives. My students deserve top billing in the gratitude department. I don't take for granted that they trusted me to guide them at such a stressful time, or their generous permission to share their personal stories and essays with future college applicants.

Along the road from finding the ideal editor who believed in my mission, to writing and revising *College Essay Confidence*, to the publication journey, I collected precious allies like others collect rare coins. Thank you to Anna Worrall and the Gernert team for always having my back. Thank you to Jason Gardner, this book's noble captain, and the team at New World Library, especially Kristen Cashman, Kim Corbin, Sandy Balin, and Tona Pearce Myers. And thank you to Cheryl Vigder Brause, Judith Craver, PhD, and Katherine Appy, PsyD, for contributing your wisdom to this book's innards (and to mine).

Gratitude abounds for Mathew Lebowitz, my ride-or-die partner, always a patient reader and a tolerant listener to my endless spitballing of ideas. The stories of my children grace some of these pages. Boundless thanks to Hannah and Ethan; you constantly wow me and fill me with admiration. Thank you to my parents, my extended family — especially Eve, Ben, Doug, Susan, and Sheila — and my community of whip-smart and compassionate friends (you know who you are) for your support, inspiration, and reassurance that crises of confidence happen to everyone.

Finally, I appreciate you, dear reader. My generation is counting on yours to nurture your talents and keep our world spinning. It felt like serious business choosing which exercises and advice to include in this book to help maximize your confidence, minimize your stress, and prepare you to lead us all into a better future. Thank you for motivating me to sit down and write.

INDEX

About the Author

Jill Margaret Shulman is the author of *College Admissions Cracked: Saving Your Kid (and Yourself) from the Madness* and founder of In Other Words, a college essay coaching service. She has spent decades shepherding families through the college admissions process and has evaluated applications at elite colleges. Shulman has also taught writing at The New School, City University of New York, and NYU and has been featured in *Forbes*, *LA Times*, *The New York Times*, *Parents*, and elsewhere. She lives in the higher education mecca of Western Massachusetts. Learn more at Jill Shulman.com.

NEW WORLD LIBRARY is dedicated to publishing books and other media that inspire and challenge us to improve the quality of our lives and the world.

We are a socially and environmentally aware company. We recognize that we have an ethical responsibility to our readers, our authors, our staff members, and our planet.

We serve our readers by creating the finest publications possible on personal growth, creativity, spirituality, wellness, and other areas of emerging importance. We serve our authors by working with them to produce and promote quality books that reach a wide audience. We serve New World Library employees with generous benefits, significant profit sharing, and constant encouragement to pursue their most expansive dreams.

We print our books with soy-based ink on paper from sustainably managed forests. We power our Northern California office with solar energy, and we respectfully acknowledge that it is located on the ancestral lands of the Coast Miwok Indians. We also contribute to nonprofit organizations working to make the world a better place for us all.

Our products are available wherever books are sold.

customerservice@NewWorldLibrary.com
Phone: 415-884-2100 or 800-972-6657
Orders: Ext. 110
Fax: 415-884-2199
NewWorldLibrary.com

Scan below to access our newsletter
and learn more about our books and authors.